Praise for
The 30-Second Commute

"This book is the next best thing to having your own business coach. It is THE practical, real-life, no-nonsense reference guide to what REALLY works in starting your own home-based business."

Arnold Sanow, MBA, CSP
President, The Business Source, Inc.
Author, *Get Along with Anyone, Anytime, Anywhere:*
8 Keys to Creating Enduring Connections with
Customers, Co-Workers . . . Even Kids

"Read it! No, wait—DEVOUR it! It's everything you need to know to start your own home-based business and succeed faster!"

Dr. Wolf J. Rinke, CSP
Author, *Make It a Winning Life:*
Success Strategies for Life,
Love and Business

"If you've lacked the courage to start your own home business, worry no more, your cure has arrived! *The 30-Second Commute* is an all-inclusive book that covers every intimidating aspect about going solo. Williams and Cooper's insights into this scary journey will leave you feeling encouraged and ready to step up to embrace your passion."

Sandra Ford Walston
Author, *COURAGE: The Heart and Spirit of Every Woman*

"My home-based business has grown into a multi-million-dollar enterprise— so take it from me, *The 30-Second Commute* is an amazing book! Practical philosophies, compelling counsel, and insightful ideas all presented in a style that will move you to take action and make your dream of a home-based business a reality!"

Scott McKain
Vice Chairman, Obsidian Enterprises
Author, *ALL Business Is Show Business!*

"This is a 'must read' for anyone starting or operating their own business. Williams and Cooper present so many practical strategies, ideas, and resources you'll be saying, 'Why didn't I think of that myself' the entire time you read this. Your copy is guaranteed to be dog-eared and tattered as you refer back to this invaluable reference over and over again as your business endeavor evolves."

Vilis Ozols
Author, *Motivational Leaders*
and *Motivational Selling*

"*The 30-Second Commute* is loaded with great ideas and money-saving techniques. This book will save you from many painful mistakes and knock several years off your learning curve."

Rick Ott
Author, *Creating Demand*

"Williams and Cooper have done an outstanding job of simplifying the complex process of successful home-based business start-up."

Chris Hansen
2003 U.S. Small Business Administration
"Home Business Advocate of the Year"

"A 30-second commute? What a great concept! Williams and Cooper have delivered a realistic, practical, comprehensive, and fun-to-read guide to working from home."

Bill Cates
Author, *Get More Referrals Now*

"While the path of your 30-second commute may sound easy, it can be fraught with U-turns and potholes without the right road map. Beverley Williams and Don Cooper have taken this path so many mornings that they've cleared the way and smoothed the bumps for others to follow. Use your copy of *The 30-Second Commute*—filled with practical, sensible, hard-earned tips—to chart a quick and safe path for your new life today."

Lisa Roberts
The Entrepreneurial Parent
www.en-parent.com

"Invaluable advice and insights from two nationally known entrepreneurs. They don't tell you to climb the ladder to your own success. They show you how to take the ELEVATOR to the top!"

George-Anne Fay
Author, *Will the Real Boss Please Stand Up?*

"As a self-employed entrepreneur, I've considered writing a 'how to' book myself. What a relief to find Williams and Cooper's book more complete and detailed than I could have envisioned. It's a keeper for anyone in a home business."

Paul O. Radde, Ph.D.
Author, *Thrival! How to Have an Above Average Day Every Day*

The 30-Second Commute

The Ultimate Guide to Starting and Operating a Home-Based Business

Beverley Williams

Don Cooper

McGraw-Hill
New York   Chicago   San Francisco
Lisbon   London   Madrid   Mexico City
Milan   New Delhi   San Juan   Seoul
Singapore   Sydney   Toronto

1 2 3 4 5 6 7 8 9 0   AGM/AGM   0 9 8 7 6 5 4

ISBN: 0-07-142406-7

The publication is designed to provide accurate and authoritative information in regard to the subject matter covered. It is sold with the understanding that neither the author nor the publisher is engaged in rendering legal, accounting, futures/securities trading, or other professional service. If legal advice or other expert assistance is required, the services of a competent professional person should be sought.

—From a Declaration of Principles jointly adopted by a Committee
of the American Bar Association and a Committee of Publishers.

McGraw-Hill books are available at special quantity discounts to use as premiums and sales promotions, or for use in corporate training programs. For more information, please write to the Director of Special Sales, McGraw-Hill Professional, Two Penn Plaza, New York, NY 10121-2298. Or contact your local bookstore.

Library of Congress Cataloging-in-Publication Data

Williams, Beverley.
    The 30-second commute: The ultimate guide to starting and operating a
    home-based business / by Beverley Williams and Don Cooper.
        p.   cm.
    ISBN 0-07-142406-7 (pbk. : alk. paper)
    1. Home-based business—Management.   2. New business enterprises.   I. Title:
    Thirty-second commute.   II. Cooper, Don.   III. Title
    HD62.5 38.W55 2004
    658.4'012—dc22   2003024378

This book is printed on recycled, acid-free paper containing a minimum of 50% recycled, de-inked fiber.

To my husband, John, without whom none of this would have been possible. Without his love, support and understanding I wouldn't be where I am or who I am today.

Bev Williams

To my father, Kenneth Cooper, who taught me that anything is possible if you refuse to give up.

Don Cooper

Contents

Foreword

As a guy who has worked at home since 1971, I'm very impressed at how simple it has been made by Beverley Williams and Don Cooper in this book. I'd have given almost anything for the information in *The 30-Second Commute* before I embarked upon my own home-based ventures.

It could have saved me countless hours, endless mistakes, and earned limitless money for me. But I did it the hard way. Beverley and Don tell you the easy way to learn what took me over 30 years to figure out.

They not only give you a highly perceptive overview of what working at home entails, they also attend to all the details, and those details are what can make or break you.

Entrepreneurs, being free spirits, often overlook very important factors because they are so passionate about their business idea. If you're going to succeed at your home-based venture, you can't overlook any of these factors. But working at home is a pure joy if you do it right.

This is the book that tells you exactly how to do it right.

One of the things that most impresses me about *The 30-Second Commute* is its comprehensiveness. It tells you things you'd never learn at the Harvard Business School, or any other school for that matter. These guys have done it themselves, so they are talking reality more than theory. And believe me, when you're commuting in your slippers, theory doesn't matter. Reality is all that counts.

As the author of umpteen books on marketing, I paid extra close attention to their chapter on marketing. Guess what? They haven't left out one thing. They've revealed a galaxy of extremely low-cost methods of getting the right word out to the right people in the right way.

Working at home does not imply laziness. It actually requires a lot of energy. But it's far easier than you may think, and it's even easier once you've wrapped your mind around the words you're about to read in this book.

Beverley and Don are able to take complex thoughts and present them in a clear and readable manner. If I had a huge company, I'd quake in my boots with the fear that some of my employees might discover this book, and with it, a whole new way of life.

I must admit that working from home is far more joyous than you'd probably ever imagine. I say this after spending 12 years in large corporations and loving every moment of those years. But those years were bland and unexciting compared with the bliss of working at home, calling my own shots, and earning far more than I ever earned as a senior vice president with the largest advertising agency in the world.

Best of all, my 47-year-old marriage continues to thrive, and I didn't miss out on one moment of my child's growing up. Those are only some of the fringe benefits of working from home sweet home.

Still, I had to figure it all out for myself, groping in the dark, and making things up as I went along. Armed with a road map, such as this one, I would have attained my goals much more rapidly and taken a lot fewer Tums on the way to success.

The only regret that you'll have after completing *The 30-Second Commute* is that you didn't read it five years ago and that Beverley and Don didn't write it ten years ago. It will give you a major head start on your quest for freedom and balance, financial independence, and inner satisfaction.

Jay Conrad Levinson
Author, *Guerrilla Marketing*

Acknowledgments

We'd like to thank our editorial team at McGraw-Hill—Stephen Isaacs, Ann Wildman, and Barry Neville—for all their support, hard work, and vision. We'd also like to thank our agents, Michael Larsen and Elizabeth Pomada, two of the best in the business and great friends to boot.

Jim Blasingame and Dorie McCubbrey provided us with a tremendous amount of advice, insight, and encouragement, for which we are deeply grateful.

Thanks also to all our friends in the National Speakers Association for your encouragement, ideas, and laughter. And a special thank you to everyone who has ever been a member of the American Association of Home-Based Businesses. Together we've helped shape an industry.

Introduction

Parts of this book were written at a construction site where Bev and her husband, John, are building a log home in the mountains of western Maryland. Parts of this book were written on Don's deck looking out over the beautiful mountains of Colorado. Parts of this book were written on airplanes. And parts of this book were written in all manner of unusual places and locales.

The advances in technology in the last 10 to 15 years allow anyone to work anywhere at anytime dressed any way they want to dress. Laptops, cell phones, fax machines, e-mail, the Internet—all have made it possible for millions of people to own a business of their own from the comfort of their home and anywhere else they decide to work.

Whether you're employed by corporate America or are a stay-at-home mom or dad, you probably know people who are running a business from their home right in your own neighborhood. Millions of people dream about having their own business, and home is now the most popular place to have that business. In May 2003, a report published by the Office of Advocacy of the Small Business Administration titled "Small Business by the Numbers" stated that 52 percent of all small businesses were home-based. It also indicated that the number of men and women who own home-based businesses are about equal.

Why do so many people consider a home-based business to be their best option? The most common reasons people give for starting a business from home are:

- Tired of commuting two to three hours a day in heavy traffic
- Want to spend more time with family
- Low start-up costs
- More relaxed work atmosphere

The 30-Second Commute   The advantages of not having to commute more than 30 seconds are wonderful. You don't have to fight traffic. You don't have to go to the office several hours earlier than usual in order to avoid the heaviest traffic. There's less wear and tear on your car. There's less wear and tear on you. The only downside is that it's difficult to convince someone you can't get to the office because of bad weather.

More Time with Your Family   Many working parents complain that they don't get to see their children, and sometimes spouses, because they have to leave for work so early in the morning, when everyone else is still asleep. Others complain about missing their children's school activities, extracurricular sports games and other milestones because it's difficult to get away from work.

Schools used to be able to rely on mothers to volunteer to help with special activities and field trips, but today it's difficult for parents who work outside the home to commit to regular volunteer hours. Home-based business owners have more flexibility when it comes to using their time, and some of that time can be used to volunteer for children's school and extra-curricular activities.

Low Start-Up Costs   Think about the cost of starting a business in commercial space. First you have to find a suitable location that you can afford. Next, you have to commit to a monthly rent and utilities. Then you have to furnish it with "suitable" office furnishings, and put in a phone system.

A home-based business start-up finds space within the house, arranges the family furniture to furnish the office, uses the phone or a cell phone for the business or adds a second number to the existing house line—and you're ready to go! This one is a no-brainer! You can use your financial resources to buy the best equipment, remodel for your office space, and do marketing. It's a much better use of your money than paying rent and utilities for a place outside the home.

A More Relaxed Work Atmosphere   Now let's compare going to work in a corporate office or commercial space with working in your home-based business.

When you leave your house in the morning to go to work, even if your company has a casual work attire policy, you still have to spend time getting ready. Taking the travel time in your morning routine into account, it's not unlikely that you'll watch the morning news to see what the traffic and weather are like. You may decide to pack a lunch that day. Maybe you have to rush around so much getting ready that you don't get your second cup of coffee, so you fill up a travel mug to take with you. By the time you get into your car to commute to work, you probably feel as if you've already put in half a day. And by the time you get to your office, it might feel as if you've already put in a whole day's work!

Now imagine getting up in the morning, starting the coffee, taking a leisurely shower, putting on some casual clothes, eating your breakfast while reading the paper, and then taking a dozen or so steps to your office. You're now at work. No stress. No hassle. No traffic. A much more relaxed way to arrive in your office.

THE CHANGING REALITIES OF WORK

For more than 15 years, Beverley has been a home-based business owner and an advocate for working at home. In the beginning she was scoffed at, laughed at, and just plain considered crazy for speaking out in favor of home-based businesses. In fact, in the late 1970s most people believed that home-based business owners were either little old ladies crocheting items for a local consignment store or people who couldn't get a "real" job.

Times certainly have changed. In March 2000, a Small Business Administration report, "The Hidden Economy," included the following highlights:

- Over 55,000 home-based businesses had sales of more than $1 million in 1992.
- Average receipts of all home-based firms was about $40,000.
- Forty to 44 percent of all home-based businesses required less than $5,000 for start-up.
- One-third of all home-based businesses used personal assets to start, and 46 percent used personal savings.
- Fewer than 5 percent of home-based businesses eventually move out of the home.
- Owners of home-based businesses work, on average, 26 to 35 hours per week.
- Most full-time home-based business owners work at least 40 hours a week.
- Over half of all home-based businesses survive at least five years.

CHANGING YOUR LIFE AT HOME

Why write another how-to home-based business book? Because information changes, and because we feel that starting and operating a home-based business has not yet been fully explained.

Understanding who you are and what motivates you to be a home-based business owner versus a commercial space–based business owner is where we'll begin. The first chapter, "Trading In Your Suit," will help you determine if you have the "right stuff" to make it work, as well as help you decide what type of business you want to run from your home.

As important as what you do is what you're allowed to do by zoning. Many potential home-based business owners make the mistake of assuming they can do anything they want in their own home. Not so! Chapter 2, "Getting into the Zone," presents the questions you need to ask, who you need to ask them of, and what to do if you don't like the answers.

Once you've determined you can legally operate a business from your home, you need to know whether licenses are necessary, what taxes you'll have to pay, and what the best form of business is for you. Chapter 3, "Keeping It Legal," provides extensive information to get you up and running your business—legally, while keeping as much of your hard-earned money as you can.

Knowing where you're going and how you're going to get there will make the difference between success and failure. Mapping out your plan of business isn't as hard as most people think, yet few people spend the time to do a plan. In Chapter 4, "Mapping Your Route to Success," you'll learn how to write a plan that includes integrating your personal and professional lives while running a successful business.

Maxing out your credit cards is not the best way to finance a home-based business. In the past it has been the only option for some start-ups because financing the small amount of money required for a home-based business start-up was something banks and other financial institutions just didn't do. They believed that the return on their time was too small to make it worthwhile. Now, there are other options, and in general a different attitude by some less traditional finance institutions. Chapter 5, "Piggy Banks and Megabanks," discusses your options for financing, from breaking open the piggy bank to microbusiness financing.

Once you have the basics in place to start your business, where in the house will you set up your office? Chapter 6, "A Corner Office or a Corner of the Dining Room?" helps you understand the impact on your family and your family's normal household routines of where you put your office.

Now that you have a place to work, what else do you need? Technology has made it possible to work from home, but what technology should you have for your business? Chapter 7, "Outfitting a High-Tech Home Office," will walk you through the choices and help you understand what's right for you.

Now put on your hat and get to work. What hat you say? That's a good question, and the answer will vary with the job you're doing at the time. Regardless of what else you do, you're now the CEO of your own company and the hats you wear are numerous. Chapter 8, "Starting at the Top," helps you understand which hat to wear when, and what hat to pass off to someone else when you can.

Managing your time when you're a home-based business owner is a real challenge. It may seem like you'll have more time to do more things, but there are still only 24 hours in any given day. In Chapter 9, "Managing Your Time, Your Life, and Your Sanity," you'll find tips on making the most of the time you have as well as finding the right balance for you between personal time and business time.

Marketing is one of the most challenging issues any small business owner faces. For home-based business owners, the additional challenge is having a nontraditional office that doesn't have walk-by traffic and isn't in the normal business district. So how do you let your market know you're there? Chapter 10, "Getting the World to Beat a Path to Your Door," tells you all you need to know to market your business.

But what happens when you no longer have someone else in the office to bounce your ideas off? The answer is as close as Chapter 11, "What Happened to the Water Cooler?" Creating your own support system for those times when you really need to hear another human voice is what dealing with isolation is all about.

And what about your family? Will they work with you in the business? Formally or informally, Chapter 12, "Making It a Family Affair," explains how to make the most of your family's interest in being your employee of the month.

Chapter 13, "Where Do I Go from Here?" helps you understand how your business can grow, if that's what you want to do. How it can grow, why you would want it to grow, and who to grow it with will be covered.

Growth may mean more business than you can handle alone. Do you hire employees or contract out some of the work? Chapter 14, "Employees or Independent Contractors?" explains the difference between an employee and an independent contractor and how to avoid trouble with the IRS.

And, finally, at the end of the book, in "But Wait, There's More!" we'll provide contact information for government agencies that work with and for small and home-based businesses, organizations that can help you as a small business owner, insurance companies that offer in-home business policies, and books on a wide variety of subjects pertinent to home-based businesses.

When you start a business in your home, you're creating a brand new lifestyle for yourself and perhaps for your family. This book will help you not only decide on and start a home-based business, but will prepare you for the new way of life you'll be creating along with your new business.

Chapter 1

TRADING IN YOUR SUIT

How to Get Started

Whether you're employed by corporate America or you're a stay-at-home Mom or Dad, you probably know people who are running a business from their home right in your own neighborhood. Millions of people dream about having their own business, and as we noted in the Introduction, home is now the most popular place to have that business.

We've already listed the most common reasons people consider a home-based business a terrific option: an aversion to long commutes, a desire to spend more time with family, the low start-up costs, and a more relaxed work atmosphere. Now let's discuss what it takes to be a home-based entrepreneur and how to choose a business that fits your desired life and family style.

WHAT IT TAKES TO WORK AT HOME

What are the personality traits of a home-based entrepreneur? It takes a person who:

- Is self-motivated
- Is a self-starter
- Has good time management skills
- Is able to set priorities
- Has small business management skills
- Has marketing skills
- Has finance skills
- Has good networking skills

What if you don't have any or all of these skills? You can learn them. This book will help you learn many of these skills and offers resources for more help. The key to being successful in a small, home-based business is to give yourself the time to learn what you need to learn and plan what you need to plan. Not taking the time to learn is the biggest cause of failure for any small business.

Some traits that are important to be an entrepreneur are:

- Competitiveness
- A positive, confident attitude
- Resourcefulness
- Creativity
- Persistence

It's not impossible to learn these traits, but it will help if you are already a fairly confident, resourceful person.

Some of the most common business mistakes include:

- Not having a plan
- Not evaluating the market effectively
- Poor time management
- Trying to appeal to everyone
- Insufficient start-up capital
- Charging the wrong price

Information we present in the following chapters will help you avoid these mistakes.

Remember, also, that when you start and operate a business from home, you are not just starting a new business—you're creating a new lifestyle for yourself and your household. You will have much more flexibility in how you spend your time. You'll be able to mix business errands with personal errands to make the most effective use of your time. You will find the right balance between your personal and professional life.

How do you become a home-based business owner and create this new lifestyle for yourself? Follow your passions.

WHAT KIND OF BUSINESS WILL YOU BE?

You may have an idea for a business, or just a desire to work from home, or maybe both. Perhaps it's a skill you want to utilize, a hobby you want to work at full-time, or an idea for a better mousetrap. Whether you're trying to decide what kind of business to operate from home full-time or part-time or already have a business idea, here are some things you should look at:

- Your knowledge
- Your skills
- Your personality
- Your passion
- Your financial needs
- Your local zoning ordinances

Although zoning ordinances is last on the list, it's the first thing you need to investigate. You must check zoning on numerous levels depending on your area. Don't assume you can do what you want in your own home. More than one neighbor has turned in a home-based business owner for operating illegally just out of spite. It is a waste of your time, energy, and resources to start a business in your home before checking out the regulations. In Chapter 2, "Getting into the Zone," we'll discuss zoning in detail. If you have not yet checked into zoning, read that chapter now and come back after you've investigated the legality of operating a business from your home.

So let's go back to the other five items in the list, your knowledge, your skills, your personality, your passion, and your financial needs.

You'll notice that each item starts with the word YOUR. *You* are the business, so what you know, how you think, and what makes you get excited are essential to the type of business you operate.

We're often asked about a business that will make the owner money, as if that were the only thing that mattered. There is nothing wrong with making money; however, it's frustrating to try to answer this question without knowing a person's skills, personality, knowledge, and passion. The book *Do What You Love—The Money Will Follow* by Marsha Sinetar has a lot of merit. It may not always happen if you don't plan properly; but with time and effort, the money will come from just about any endeavor if a person's skills, knowledge, personality, and passions are involved.

Your Passions, Your Knowledge, and Your Skills

So what do you love to do? Remember in school when you took an aptitude test and then your school counselor told you what field you should go into? Many people found those test results too limiting, given their ambitions. There are no limits now. If you're at the point of asking yourself what kind of business you should start at home, it's time to take a different kind of aptitude test—one that has no limits that you don't set yourself.

So where do you start testing your aptitude? With a pencil, paper, and quiet space. Draw a line vertically down the center of the paper. At the top, head the columns "Love to Do" and "Hate to Do." You'll notice these are stronger words than *like* and *don't like*. That's because you want to bring out your passions.

Some of what you love to do might involve helping other people or designing clothes or going shopping or building furniture. Try to be as specific as possible. For instance, helping other people is pretty broad. What kind of help? Help by providing meals, making phone calls, providing day care, giving advice? To whom? The elderly, the sick, new parents, the physically challenged, small business owners, major corporations?

The most popular types of businesses that are frequently run from home include:

- *Consulting:* marketing, financial, management, government contracting, technology, customer service
- *Services:* desktop publishing, accounting/bookkeeping, medical transcription, business plan writing, cleaning services, personal coaching, fitness training, massage therapy, computer repair, editorial services, senior citizen services, import/export, medical billing, professional organizing, pet sitting, Web design, wedding coordination

As you can see, this list, though by no means complete, is extensive and hits just about every type of field you can imagine.

Once you've decided what you love to do, try to apply your skills. Are you a fast and accurate typist? Do you have good phone skills? Do you have a degree in special education or nursing? Do you have experience in a field where companies are outsourcing that work?

Consider talking with a close friend about what they see as your skills. The strengths others see in you may come as a surprise to you or may confirm your own feelings. In the book *Wishcraft* by Barbara Sher there is an exercise in which you set up a get-together with two or three friends and have them talk about you as if you weren't there. They talk about your strengths and weaknesses while you take notes. Bev did this a number of years ago while trying to decide upon a new direction for her home-based business. Although it was difficult to listen to others talk about her as if she wasn't there, she was somewhat surprised at what they had to say and it helped her refocus her business plan. Afterward, Bev began a new home-based business journey into professional speaking. Without the insight from her trusted friends, she might have continued floundering around.

Once you've begun to narrow down your "Love to Do" list to the top five or six things, and have determined that you have marketable skills for those items, let the ideas sit for a while. The ideas will become clearer in time; you may find that something you thought you would like to do no longer appeals to you.

We all have a tendency to look only at the positives when we're excited about an idea. After a few days, look at your list again and reevaluate your ideas. On a separate piece of paper, write down the top few. Now make a column for the negatives about each one and a column for information needed. For instance, you love to cook and help the elderly, so you've decided you might like to provide a meal service to them. The first negative may be that you don't know if you'd need special licenses to prepare food for others to consume. In the "Information Needed" column you might write down: "Call the Department of Licenses and Inspection and the Health Department."

If you want to consult with large corporations on government contracting but aren't sure which agencies would use your particular area of expertise, your "Negative" column notation might say: "Lack information on how many corporations in this area do business with the government that would require my services." Under your "Information Needed" column you would write: "Research corporations who want to obtain government contracts." You may (and probably will have) more than one or two negatives in a column for the same field. Don't let a long list discourage you. Now you at least have a to-do list to get you started.

There are lots of places where you can learn what you need to know. Start with your local library for books that pertain to your weak areas. Look in the self-help section for books on self-discipline, coming out of your shell, or understanding why you are shy around others, if that's the case.

Check the small business section for books about entrepreneurship. You'll find books on incorporating yourself, writing a business plan, bookkeeping, marketing, networking, and just about anything else you need to know.

In the reference section of the library you will find the *Directory of Associations*. Look for the associations in the field you're interested in. You may be able to photocopy a page of the directory; otherwise, copy the contact information. Write the associations or look at their Web sites for information that could be helpful to you. Many associations list other resources or have seminars and workshops you may be able to attend.

There are numerous resources that can help you decide on a home-based business. One of the best is a book by Paul and Sarah Edwards titled *Best Home Businesses for the 21st Century* (published by Tarcher/Putnam). It lists 95 businesses that are successfully run from a home office, and under each there's a brief description of the business, knowledge and skills needed, start-up costs, advantages and disadvantages, pricing and potential earnings, a best estimate of the market potential, the best way to market that business, first steps, and additional resources. This is a truly remarkable resource for beginning the journey to your own home-based business. Even if it doesn't list the type of business you're currently thinking about, you may find a similar business, or something entirely different, that appeals to you.

Another resource is *Home Business: The Home-Based Entrepreneur's Magazine* (www.homebusinessmag.com) a bimonthly publication that publishes an annual list of the top 250 home businesses. They range from franchises to multilevel marketing companies. The magazine includes such information as company names, addresses, and phone numbers, as well as start-up costs and the kind of support provided.

Because computers have become so commonplace in households, and are now the basis for a lot of home-based businesses, we also recommend another book by Paul and Sarah Edwards, *Making Money with Your Computer at Home* (second edition). The first half of this book lists 100 businesses you can run from a home computer, while the second half gives you some insight on how to get started.

After reading and researching some of your business ideas, you may feel overwhelmed by some of the hats you'll have to wear in your business. Chapter 8, "Starting at the Top," covers what some of those hats are and how to handle them. Even if you decide to turn over some of the work to others, it's essential to have a basic understanding of what it takes to run a business. You don't need an MBA, but you will need some knowledge. Check with your local college's Department of Continuing Education for small business course offerings. Most are short courses. Others are a group of courses that will teach you what you need to know about running any small business. One of the advantages of taking these courses—besides learning how to run a small business—is meeting others who also want to start a small business. Don't be surprised to find that half or more of them are starting their own home-based businesses.

The Department of Education in your area may also have an Adult Education program. Many of these offer small business classes as well. The advantage to Continuing Education programs and Adult Education programs is that they're taught by people with real-life experience in the field and it makes the class much more interesting.

Look in the blue government pages of your telephone book for the Office of Economic Development (OED). One of their functions is to help businesses in the area. They can provide you with some market research, workshops, and other resources. They want your business to succeed, so they will provide you with lots of information about other resources, the economic climate in your area, and there may even be a mentoring program you can get involved in.

There are numerous other resources listed in *But Wait, There's More,* in the back of this book, to get you started and focused on your new venture.

Okay. To this point, let's say you have acknowledged your knowledge, your skills, and your passions. Now we should look at your personality and financial needs, which are also vital to your success.

Your Personality

What does it take to be a home-based business owner besides a passion for what you want to do and the skills to do it? It takes a person who is self-motivated, has good time management skills, is able to set priorities, can handle finances, and isn't afraid to talk with people about what they do.

Here are some questions to ask yourself about being an entrepreneur:

1. Are you going into business for yourself out of desperation?
2. Are you afraid of failing?
3. Are you afraid of succeeding?
4. Are you creative?
5. Are you afraid to take risks?
6. Can you set goals and achieve them?
7. Are you prepared to give up a regular paycheck?
8. Are you willing to give up or find the financial means to pay for your own benefits?
9. Are you able to speak in public?
10. Do you know your weaknesses?
11. Do you know your strengths?
12. Is your family enthusiastic about your business idea?
13. Are you comfortable about working on your own?
14. Are you intimidated about learning something new?
15. Are you a leader?

It should be obvious to you that your answers will determine whether or not to enter into entrepreneurship. But not every answer will be a right or wrong one for entrepreneurship. For instance, question 12 about family enthusiasm may not be something you have investigated, but you will certainly need, if nothing else, a cheering squad to help you over the rough times. Having a family that encourages you makes a big difference. Having a family that doesn't support your efforts can undermine your efforts.

Being able to speak in public (question 9) may not be something you're comfortable with now, but it's something you can learn by doing. Not that you need to become a professional speaker and always speak in front of a group. However, it is important to be able to speak easily about your business to others. We'll cover more on networking and marketing skills in Chapter 10, "Getting the World to Beat a Path to Your Door."

If you're the type who needs someone to tell you what to do each day, *don't start your own business*. On the other hand, if you're a leader, the type who always ends up as the head of a committee, the one everyone else comes to for problem solving, the one who's always coming up with a new or better way to accomplish a project, you may just be self-motivated enough to own your own business. It takes energy and spirit to start and operate a business in your home. No one else is going to be there to give you direction. You may have to look in the mirror to see a friendly face. If this doesn't appeal to you, spruce up your résumé and begin looking for another job to add excitement to your life.

You must be willing and able to wear all the hats in your business. As a home-based business owner, you will be the CEO, the bookkeeper, the marketing department, the supply buyer, the file clerk, and the janitor. You'll need good time management skills. If you're not good at managing your time now, you can learn. Chapter 9, "Managing Your Time, Your Life, and Your Sanity," covers this in more detail.

FINANCIAL NEEDS

Everyone wants to make money from his or her efforts. How many times have you seen an ad or heard an infomercial about a home-based business that would make you thousands of dollars in your first month of business? It sounds so believable. For most people, though, it's not reality. We'll explore how to check out these business opportunities a little later in the chapter. For now, let's look realistically at how much money you need and how much more you want from your business efforts.

Full-Time or Part-Time?

How many hours a week can you realistically devote to your business from home? For some that answer will be determined by whether they're still employed. For many, starting a part-time home-based business in the evenings and weekends while employed elsewhere is a way to test the waters of a new business. No one else can decide this for you.

The most common reasons for starting a full-time home-based business are:

- Being laid off, downsized, or fired from a job
- Fear of being laid off, downsized, or fired from a job
- Dissatisfaction with working for someone else and wanting to be your own boss
- Qualifying to retire with benefits but not ready for a rocking chair
- Tired of commuting
- Wanting to spend more time with family

You may see yourself in these most commonly stated reasons or you may have a different one. Whatever your reasons for wanting to start a home-based business of your own, understand that it will be hard work, and that it may take up to three years to make the kind of money you expect to make from your own business. It will not necessarily be a nine-to-five, 40-hour-a-week job. That will be your choice. However, it will be your new way of life because your whole life will change. It will not be just what you do, but who you are.

Some people start a part-time home-based business in order to earn extra money and never expect it to be a full-time endeavor. Others start a part-time business while still working full-time in order to continue their employee benefits. Still others start part-time to test the waters of a business idea to make sure it will work before giving up the comforts of employment. If your income is essential to your household, a part-time business is the smartest way to start.

The most common question asked by those starting or operating a part-time business while still employed full-time is: "When should I quit my day job to make this a full-time business?" You will be the best judge of that, but here are some things to look for:

- You're making more money at your part-time business than you are being employed.
- You're taking time off your day job to work at your part-time business because you have so much business.
- You're making enough money part-time that you can't take on any more business and you have clients waiting for you to have the time.
- You're making enough money to pay for your own benefit programs.

Remember that when you quit your job, you will no longer have the benefits you may have enjoyed as an employee. You and your business will now have to pay for everything. Even though it may seem as if you're making more money, you'll have more expenses. We'll go into finance issues in more detail later in this chapter and in Chapters 5 and 6.

People who have decided to use their current job skills to create a part-time business of their own account for about half of the home-based business start-ups. There are some advantages and disadvantages and some other issues when it comes to staying in your current field of work:

Advantages
- You already have the knowledge you need to begin.
- You have instant credibility because of experience in the field.

Disadvantages
- You may be in direct competition with your current employer, which could jeopardize your current position.
- You will be doing your "job" more hours than you might like.

Other Issues
If you're okay with the disadvantages, let's look at the other issues involved:

- Will the companies you want to attract as clients expect your services to be available to them during "normal" business hours?
- Do you have flexible hours that would allow you to work at your home-based business for a few hours in the morning before going to your full-time job?
- You may need to spend time gathering information for a particular client; can you do this outside of your employed hours?
- What about the client's work? Can you pick up and deliver outside your employed hours?

If none of this is pertinent to your business, then you may not have any problems. For instance, if you do research on the Web or do freelance writing, your hours of work are flexible enough to do in the evenings and on weekends. Therefore, it won't interfere with your full-time employment.

If you're concerned about being in direct competition with your current employer, think about what's missing in the goods or services being offered by the company.

What do clients sometimes ask for that your present employer doesn't offer, perhaps because it is not cost effective for a larger business to provide it?

Is there a different method for delivering the same services?

Can you provide this service independently without risking your current employment?

In other words, *can you find a need and fill it?*

For those who decide to start a business that's different from the one they've been involved in as an employee, the challenges include:

- Having enough knowledge and skill to do something different
- Turning a hobby into a marketable product
- Becoming involved in a different market than you're a part of now

None of these challenges are insurmountable. It will take a little more time and research to get the business up and running. Once again, a to-do list will help you set your goals for achieving a viable business.

FINDING A BALANCE

There are only 24 hours in every day and no way to manufacture more. However, as a home-based business, you'll have more freedom in how you use those 24 hours. The key is to find a balance between your business and your personal life. Chapter 9 will help with that.

Another issue to think about is the impact on the other members of your household. If you're married, have children, or are involved with a "significant other," is this business something they can help with or will it be taking away from your time with them? Take the time to talk with the others in your life about your ideas and what possible impact you anticipate the business having on your personal relationships. Most people find their quality time with family is improved when they have a home-based business. Be assured that taking the time to communicate now will help the quality of time spent later—both on business and personal time.

What follows are a few more specifics you'll need to think about.

Staying Home with the Kids

Many mothers and mothers-to-be ask Bev about having a home-based business so they can stay home with their baby. There are also a lot of fathers choosing to stay at home with the kids while operating full- or part-time businesses from the home. In fact, there are many similarities between starting a home-based business and starting a family. There will be times when your children and your business will demand your attention at the same time.

Infants

Although some babies sleep in predictable patterns, you can't count on it to be the case with your own child. Some babies sleep in 20-minute snatches, so that just about the time you think they're settled and you can concentrate on a work project, they wake up. New mothers and fathers soon learn that when baby sleeps, they need to sleep as well. Once the infant establishes a regular sleep pattern, it will (hopefully) be a little easier to plan time for operating a business.

The reality is that it's extremely difficult to operate a full-time business and spend quality time with an infant. It's best to plan on a part-time operation until the child is school age, or to make child-care arrangements. Grandparents, nannies, live-in help are the best options, but not suitable options for everyone. If a full-time income is essential to your household, then make sure you have a budget for child care. If spending time with your infant is important, tighten your belt and make do with a part-time business for now.

Babies grow in spurts, and businesses often do the same. Think about how you'll handle the growth of both as they relate to each; for instance, as a baby begins to explore its world, you may need to adjust the location of your office equipment and space. Bev often took care of one of her grandsons when he was first born. He was placed in a portable crib next to her desk during the day. The ringer on her office phone was turned to low and she was able to accomplish a lot during his naps. He was often content to lie awake in the crib with an occasional bit of attention from Grandma. It worked well for a while. Once he began crawling and walking, he demanded full-time attention, and Bev spent more time working evenings and weekends.

As your business requires more of your time, you may need to make other arrangements to make sure baby is taken care of properly. Good organization and time management skills will help. However, you may need to plan for some day care in your home. Perhaps a neighborhood teenager can help out. Or find a child-care center that accepts drop-ins for those times when your deadlines are less flexible. Of course, you'll need to take these costs into consideration.

When your child reaches school age, you'll have more freedom to spend time on your business, while still having the flexibility to participate in school and other activities with him or her. This is one of the great advantages to having a home-based business. You aren't just starting or operating a business from home—*you are creating a new lifestyle for yourself and your family.* That means the ability to intersperse your business and personal activities.

It's certainly possible to make an income that will meet your needs and more with a small child or children at home, but it takes careful planning and some sacrifices. If you're exploring parenthood and entrepreneurship, there are a number of books that discuss how you can help balance both at the same time: *How to Raise a Family and a Career Under the Same Roof,* by Lisa Roberts, and *Mompreneurs,* by Ellen Parlapiano and Patricia Cobe. There is also At-Home Dads, a support group for men staying home with the kids while their wives work outside the home. Many of the men have a part- or full-time business as well. If you're one of the thousands of men staying home with the children while operating a business, you'll find a lot of good information at www.athomedads.com.

With planning and realistic expectations, you can soon be one of the millions of men and women who have created new lifestyles for themselves by balancing business and family under one roof.

Household Makeup

Once you have an idea of what you want to do, will having a home-based business fit your private life? We've already discussed some of the issues concerning children. But how will a home-based business impact a spouse, roommate, or significant other? It's not always easy to know in advance what the impact will be. However, discussing it now can open the lines of communication for the future. Throughout this book we'll share our personal experiences as they apply to this and other issues. Chapter 12, "Making It a Family Affair," discusses how to have family involvement in your business and what affect that may have on your personal and professional life.

Family and Friends

They may not live in your house, but if you've communicated your plans on starting a business from home to your family and friends, you might have to set some new boundaries for them.

Family and friends want to be supportive, and that's great. However, unless they're going to be instrumental in your business start-up, you'll have to limit the amount of time you spend talking on the phone or going out to lunch with them. Yes, we know we said you now have the flexibility to spend personal time as you see fit. If you decide that an hour or so a couple of days a week at lunchtime is your personal time to visit with family and friends, then so be it. However, if you find that you're constantly interrupted with phone calls while trying to concentrate on business, let the answering machine take your personal calls for a while.

This is part of the balancing act all home-based business owners must perfect, or at least practice. You have to decide how much personal interaction to intersperse with your business. Yes, you're the boss, but you also have a responsibility to your business. You won't have a business if you spend too much time on personal activities.

START-UP MONEY CONCERNS

Share your business idea with others in the household and evaluate their reaction. Allow the other(s) the opportunity to ask questions and express concerns. They may bring up issues you haven't thought about yet.

Income is the most common concern among couples who share expenses. Address this and other issues realistically:

- What will you do for financial resources until your business begins to make a profit?
- Will you have to use joint funds for your business start-up?
- How will the money be replaced?
- Will you need to borrow money to buy equipment and supplies?
- Will it be a personal loan or a business loan?
- Will you use your credit card(s) to make some purchases?
- Can you separate business from personal expenses on your statement?
- How will you make the payments?

We'll go into financing in Chapter 5, "Piggy Banks and Megabanks." However, you'll need to share your thoughts and listen to the concerns of others in the household who may be affected by your financial decisions.

If their attitude is supportive, great. If the support is not there, why not? Communication with and support of others in the household are important to your success. Try to understand their concerns, and address each one as best you can at this point. Showing that you've listened and have or will address their concerns will go a long way to assuring them you're not rushing into a business without thinking through the issues. Taking their feelings and concerns into consideration will go a long way in gaining their support. When others feel they've had input and their viewpoints have been considered, they are more likely to do all they can to help.

BUSINESS OPPORTUNITIES

Aside from designing your own business, how do you evaluate the different opportunities that seem to abound in the marketplace? How can you tell that the ones you like won't turn out to be scams? There's no surefire way to guarantee a business opportunity will make you money. But if you do your due diligence, you'll have a better chance of not getting burned by a business scam.

What Do Opportunities Look Like?

They are characterized by a large initial payment—often required before you get anything—to a company you know little about, which promises to help you develop your business and/or that has the inventory you need.

What Can Go Wrong?

- You do not earn the money that the company claims you can make—easily.
- The work is harder than you expected—the work was not made clear to you.
- There is no market for the product.
- You get no support from the company—they were friendly only before they had your money. Or the subsequent support will cost you extra.
- The company does not take your extra product back.
- The company does not back the product with warranties and guarantees, so if your customer wants his money back, you're stuck.

What Are the Warning Signs?

- Pressure to sign a contract right then, today, and pay the company a large sum of money, before you can investigate the company or its claim, or get legal advice.
- The company promises you that you can make a lot of money quickly and without much effort.
- The results are guaranteed.
- Up-front payment or fee for a kit or products or training that greatly exceeds the fair market value of the products or services.
- A fee that is payable before you receive anything in return.
- The company is unwilling to give you disclosure documents required by law (often required if the initial commitment is a payment of $500).

Often a company will tell you that you can get your money refunded after a period of time if not satisfied. Experience has shown that this is very difficult.

How Do You Investigate an Opportunity?
Ask, ask, ask!

About the Company
Ask where the company is incorporated, whether it has an office in your state, who its officers are, what their backgrounds are, and what kind of business experiences they have had. Get written copies of the company's business and financial statements. The Federal Trade Commission and some state laws require sellers of certain business opportunities to provide information about their operations to all potential purchasers.

Verify the company information. Call the Secretary of State (Corporations Division) in your state or in the state where the company is set up—ask if it's registered. If you can get a Dun & Bradstreet Report on the company, do it, or check with other business reporting services, especially to see what kinds of legal claims have been made against the company. Check with the Attorney General's Office (Consumer Affairs offices) of the state the business is registered in, or your state or county, to learn of complaints. Call the regional FTC (Federal Trade Commission) office in your area or go online to www.ftc.gov and read about specific business scams being investigated.

About the Products
Ask what the cost is to you, and what the selling price is of such products in your area. Where do you get your supply? Can you return your supply and get at least 90 percent of your money back? What performance claims can you make about the product or service? Are there guarantees and replacement or repair policies? Does the company have a method for handling complaints from either you or your customers?

Consult with people in your area. Ask whether they would buy such a product or service and what they would pay for it. Review, with persons who know your area (such as a county or city Office of Economic Development), the marketability of the product or service, the pricing, and the projected earnings.

About the Fees
What is the initial fee to pay for? Will it be escrowed? If so, by whom? Until when? If the fee covers a sample kit or initial supply of product, does it greatly exceed the cost of the kit or product?

Ask About Support

What kind of support are you supposed to get? Are there training programs? If so, are they in your area? Will there be someone you can get personal attention from? Does it cost extra? If there are others currently selling in your area, can you meet them before you commit, to check out how they're doing?

Safeguard Yourself

Get all promises in writing, and make sure the contract is signed by an authorized agent of the company. There are many business opportunity frauds out there. If it's worth your time and money to do this job, it's worth your time and money to investigate and not be pushed into a decision. You should never have to sign up the first day.

If you have reason to believe that a fraud is operating in your area, whether or not you have invested, notify your local district attorney (first), and also your consumer affairs office, your local Better Business Bureau, and the Chamber of Commerce.

COMPANIES THAT HIRE HOME-BASED WORKERS

Although this is a book about starting and operating a home-based business, it's important to address a common question about what companies hire people to work from their homes. They may really be asking about teleworking opportunities. We'll address that in a moment.

We're sure you've seen ads in your local newspapers or in e-mail messages that tell you about opportunities to work from home stuffing envelopes, assembling products, typing, and lots of other jobs. They promise you'll make money, lots of money. You may have seen signs posted at residential street corners that say you can make lots of money with your computer at home. Beware! The old saying, "If it sounds too good to be true, it probably is!" is pertinent here. Too many times you must pay for training or products that you can't do anything with. In some cases, you're purchasing a kit that tells you how to set up your own ad in order for others to call you to buy this same kit. The Federal Trade Commission (www.ftc.gov) regularly investigates such companies and rules against them as legitimate opportunities.

For instance, the envelope stuffing opportunity is one where you send in a few dollars and you get back a letter telling you to place an ad in your local paper like the one you answered. You get to keep most of the money sent in and you stuff the envelopes with the letter you received after you pay to have it copied.

The ads for the assembly of products say they will send you kits to be assembled, and when you send them back, they'll send you money. In fine print it says they will pay you after inspection of the products shows they have been done properly. They seldom are. So you've wasted your time and energy (and sometimes money to buy the kits) for nothing.

Teleworking Is Not a Business

Lots of people would like to work from home without starting their own business. The reality is, unless you already have contacts with a company, few are willing to have employees working from home without some previous employment history. It's expensive for a company to set up the telecommunications system for teleworkers. It is much more cost effective for them to hire independent consultants or small business owners to outsource their additional needs.

If, after thinking it through, you find you don't have the commitment to starting and operating a home-based business, the only option is to find employment in hopes that it might become a teleworking position in the future.

PROFESSIONAL ADVICE

We've talked a lot in this chapter about the need to check things out. In addition to the tips on how to check out a business opportunity, we highly recommend that at the beginning of any business adventure—whether starting from scratch or buying into a business opportunity—you consult with a lawyer and an accountant. Paying for an hour or two of a lawyer's and/or an accountant's time can save you money and hassles later.

A lawyer may be necessary for some types of businesses, and it pays to get acquainted with a small business lawyer in the beginning so you know whom to turn to in the event you need legal advice later, such as with contracts.

An accountant is even more valuable to you now. They can advise you on the best form of business, and how to set up your records to make sure you get the most out of your finances and pay the least amount of tax on your business income. Throughout the book we will mention the times you will need to consult either a lawyer or an accountant.

A common question is: "How do I find an accountant or a lawyer?" Here are some suggestions.

Finding an Accountant

Begin by asking other small business owners or your colleagues:

- Who they use
- What aspects they like about that person or firm
- What aspects they don't like about that person or firm
- How long they have been using the services of that person or firm

Interview each prospective accountant by asking:

- What is the profile of his or her average client?
- What type of client is his/her average client? A small business? A personal tax client?
- How extensive is his/her experience with home-based businesses? How many home-based businesses do they represent?
- What are the credentials of each prospective accountant? CPA (Certified Public Accountant)? CFA (Certified Financial Adviser)?
- What is the fee schedule? Does he/she charge for telephone calls?
- What clients would be willing to provide a reference on his/her behalf to you?

Analyze the answers by asking the following questions:

- How much of this accountant's experience matches your needs?
- How many start-up businesses have they worked with?
- Did they seem confident in answering your questions without appearing arrogant?
- Is the fee schedule affordable?
- Are the answers from their references satisfactory?

As well as listening to the actual words when you ask questions, read between the lines.

If there's no clear leader among the prospective accountants, trust your intuition! Choose the accountant with whom you felt most comfortable, and build a relationship with that person.

Your accountant may become your best business partner, saving you thousands of dollars and headaches. Your accountant will be worth every penny you spend for their services.

Finding a Lawyer

So what about a lawyer? When you choose a lawyer for your home-based business, there are several considerations to keep in mind.

Experience

You'll want a lawyer who has experience in business and commercial law. Knowledge of the substantive area of your business is also helpful. Ask the attorney to discuss his or her specialty; if the answer includes several areas of practice, the next questions should be the percentage of the practice devoted to business and commercial law. You may also want to ask the attorney how many years he's practiced in the business arena and what percent of his clients have similar legal issues.

If the school(s) attended is an important factor to you, ask the attorney where he received his undergraduate and law degrees. At a minimum, the attorney should be a member of the bar of the state in which you conduct your business; membership in voluntary local or specialty bar associations indicates a further involvement and interest in the practice of law. You may prefer hiring an attorney whose office is at home, since he would have first-hand experience in understanding the issues that face a home-based business. Many local bar associations have a secondary group just for their home-based lawyer members.

Cost

The cost of legal services is a matter of importance. Be straightforward with the attorney and ask about the hourly rate, whether a retainer or engagement fee is required if you need to contract for her services in case of a problem, and, if so, in what amount. Be sure you understand when you will be billed, when payments are due, when service charges on unpaid balances are incurred, and at what rate. Knowing these things in advance will help you make your decision. You may never need legal counsel for anything other than contracts, but it's best to have the information, just in case.

If you have a ceiling on the amount you wish to spend on a certain matter, tell the attorney as much in the initial conversation. Ask her to give you an estimate of what it will cost to have a certain issue resolved. Also, the attorney should have a written fee agreement for you to sign; you may want to ask for a copy of it before you make a final decision on whether to hire that particular attorney.

Convenience

A third consideration in choosing a lawyer is convenience. Is the attorney's office in a location convenient to you, or can he or she meet with you at your home office? What is her accessibility by phone? Ask her within what time period phone calls are returned. Most attorneys have a policy of trying to return calls within the next business day. As an indication of her responsiveness, ask the attorney for a time estimate of resolving a particular matter that you may have. For instance, if you needed a letter written by your attorney in order to collect money owed you, what kind of time frame could you expect?

Trust

Trust is also an important factor in selecting an attorney. You need to feel comfortable talking to your attorney because you'll have to reveal details that may be unfavorable to your situation. You may need to talk about finances; you will certainly have to make a full disclosure of the facts of a given situation for which you seek legal advice. Your comfort level needs to be at a point where you can discuss even very personal issues. And, it helps to *like* your attorney, because that will make your relationship more pleasant and open.

Comparison Shop

When you choose an attorney, do some comparison shopping. Call two or three and ask the questions suggested here. See how responsive they are about returning your call and what kind of treatment you receive. Pose a simple legal problem as a hypothetical and test the reaction to it.

Early Warning

Early identification of legal issues is essential. A lawyer can generally do a lot more to help you in an effective way if you engage his services before getting into an undesirable situation. For example, if you're going to enter into a contract for services, show the agreement to your attorney before signing it. If you need a contract to use with independent contractors or those you hire, ask the attorney to draft it or to review what you have drafted, *before* you actually use it. Similarly, if possible, consult an attorney before receiving papers regarding a lawsuit; go to him if a suit is merely threatened or sensed.

DO YOU OR DON'T YOU?

Now that you've reached the end of the first chapter, ask yourself this question: "Do I still want to start a home-based business?"

If the answer is yes, read on. By the time you've read this book, you will be well on your way to making your dream come true.

If the answer is no, don't be discouraged. A home-based business is not for everyone. Many have tried and given up because they lacked the discipline, they couldn't adjust to the new lifestyle, or the business was not appropriate for the home. Consider it a positive if you have decided not to start a home-based business at this time. You haven't wasted time, energy, or money starting something that would fail. You've done your homework and discovered it's not for you. Move on and pass this book on to a friend. Just remember to ask for it back at some point in time. You may discover that although this may not be the time for a home-based business, there may still be one in your future.

Chapter 2
GETTING INTO THE ZONE
Complying with
Zoning Regulations

Now that you've decided you would like to operate a business from your home, you need to find out if you're allowed by law to do so. Don't assume because it's your home that you can do what you want in it. Too many people have found out the hard way, after spending a lot of time, money, and effort, that local ordinances prohibit a business in the home. So where do you start?

Start at the highest level of governance for your area. It may be a county or province. States don't usually get involved in local governance of home-based businesses. At the local level, check first with the Department of Licenses and Inspections. The ordinances will generally be called "Home Occupation Ordinances." If they don't regulate home-based businesses, they should be able to refer you to the proper agency. In some locales the Department of Environmental Protection governs home-based businesses.

If you live within an incorporated city, check with city hall. Incorporated areas generally regulate separately from counties.

If you live in an area governed by a homeowners association, you need to read the Covenants and Restrictions (C&Rs) to determine if there are any regulations about home-based businesses. You may find these more restrictive than your local government's ordinances, especially in a tight community, that is, one that includes apartment complexes and town homes.

And, finally, if you're renting a house or apartment, read your lease carefully. If nothing is said about operating a business from the rental property, you might want to check with your landlord or management company. There may be a liability risk for the property owner if you operate a business from rental property. If this is a concern, check with your insurance agent or with an independent insurance agent—an agent who does not work for any particular insurance company but, rather, utilizes policies from several different companies—about liability insurance that would exonerate the owner(s) from your business liability. You can locate independent insurance agents in the yellow pages under "Insurance."

Throughout the country, home occupation ordinances have changed significantly over the last 20 years, mostly for the better. However, there is still a lot of work to be done to update the remaining antiquated zoning ordinances and bring them into line with twenty-first-century reality.

If you find that you are allowed to operate a business from your home, proceed to the next step. If home-based businesses are not allowed in your area, you'll have to make the decision to either move to a locale that does allow home-based businesses or try to change the ordinances.

CHANGING HOME OCCUPATION ORDINANCES

How do you change zoning ordinances to be more favorable to home-based businesses? With hard work, time, and facts.

Begin by researching whether the subject of changing home occupation ordinances has come up before. If so, why did it fail? Find out who supported the change and contact them for information. There is no sense in reinventing the wheel if someone already has information and insight on the issue.

Contact your local Chamber of Commerce to find out where they stand. Ask about members who are home-based businesses. The chamber may be willing to support your efforts by getting their members involved.

Find out how to get the item on the city or county meeting agenda and rally as much support as you can. Go to the hearing armed with as many facts and figures as possible. Be sure to address the concerns with logical, realistic plans. For instance, if increased traffic or parking is an issue, suggest that home-based businesses be allowed as long as there are no client visits.

If the problem is with your local homeowners association, changing the Covenants and Restrictions is much more difficult. Most housing communities built by residential builders follow the rules and regulations set forth by the state government's real estate division. That division supplies the builders with fill-in-the-blank C&Rs for the development. The builders simply insert the appropriate information for that community, and everything else is already in place. In order to change the C&Rs, it is necessary to get a majority—and in some cases 100 percent agreement—on changes. This is extremely difficult to do.

If your C&Rs prohibit or severely restrict home-based businesses, ask for a special exception hearing and go armed with information about the benefits of home-based businesses in that community (see "Seven Reasons to Allow Home-Based Businesses" below). Don't forget to realistically address the negatives. Once again, most opposition will be to increased traffic and parking issues. Go to the hearing with a plan on how that will be handled. For instance, if your business will not require you to have clients come to your home office, make that clear at the hearing. If the problem is with your lease, talk with your landlord about your business. Find out if there are concerns that you can do something about, such as client traffic, noise, or other common issues. Most home-based businesses are what we call "silent" businesses. There is no outward sign of a business being operated in that location. Technology often allows a home-based business to operate without any negative impact on a residential neighborhood.

Times are changing in favor of home-based businesses, but there is still opposition. Address the issues in a cool-headed, factual manner and you have a good chance of success. If you can't get the ordinance changed, ask for a special exception hearing. Perhaps your business will be allowed if taken on an individual basis.

Seven Reasons to Allow Home-Based Businesses
1. Neighborhoods with home-based businesses are safer places for children of two working parents because there is a good chance that there's someone in a nearby home in an emergency.
2. For those home offices with a view of the neighborhood, the comings and goings of strangers can be observed and suspicious activities reported to the authorities.
3. Less traffic on the highways during the "normal" rush hour.
4. Money earned is spent in the local neighborhood, helping to boost local economies.
5. It keeps jobs in the local community.
6. Decreases unemployment.
7. Provides a wider volunteer base for our communities.

MODEL ZONING ORDINANCES FOR HOME OCCUPATIONS

Many jurisdictions look for models when making changes to zoning ordinances. The following information is meant to be a guideline for today's home occupation zoning ordinances.

The home-based business is secondary to the use of the dwelling as a residence and does not change the residential character of the dwelling or lot in any visible manner. It is the primary residence of the business owner(s).

1. No noise, odor, or vibration transmits beyond the property lines (or walls in the case of multifamily dwellings).
2. The home office has no visible signs from the street that are inconsistent with signs allowed elsewhere by zoning ordinance. (A small plaque or sign by the door used by the public to enter the office is unobtrusive and often helpful to clients and delivery personnel.)
3. The home-based business has sufficient off-street parking for both residential and business use.
4. The number of businesses operated in the same dwelling shall not exceed 45 percent of the dwelling space, but more than one business may operate if the principals of the business are residents of the dwelling.
5. In areas of high-density housing, one nonresident employee may be allowed. In low-density housing areas, it is not usually necessary to regulate employees.
6. In areas of high-density housing, the number of vehicles coming to a residence for business purposes may be limited. In low-density housing areas, it is not usually necessary to regulate traffic.
7. Storage of merchandise for sale can be limited to temporary storage as in the case of direct-sales companies. Craft sales could be allowed with appropriate parking accommodations.
8. Businesses such as day-care centers, health professionals, repair shops, etc., should be regulated by separate ordinances.
9. Requiring registration of a home-based business can be both beneficial and harmful. Registration will give the local jurisdiction some indication of the number of home-based businesses in the area and awareness of their activities. On the other hand, many home-based business owners will simply ignore the requirement for numerous reasons. If you require home-based business owners to register, commit to securing the information so that they will not be inundated with unsolicited mail.

What is not appropriate for a home-based business is anything that needs a storefront, makes noise, produces an odor, or creates a fire hazard.

An auto repair shop in your garage in a close community will not be met with favor by neighbors or governments. If you live on 20 acres in the country, it might be just fine.

Prior to the Internet, retail sales were not appropriate for home-based businesses. If your business idea is to sell things over the Internet, you may be fine as long as you don't need to warehouse a large inventory. Most ordinances do not allow storage of products unless they are ordered for a specific customer. This allows the products to come in and go right back out again, as is the case with Mary Kay Cosmetics and Tupperware. However, if you buy large lots of merchandise to sell over eBay, you will need to store it someplace other than your residence to meet most local ordinances.

If you need to store merchandise for shipping Internet orders, consider renting a storage unit nearby. Make sure you factor this cost into your pricing. Make sure it is close to your home office as well. You don't want or need to be spending all your time traveling to your storage unit. Depending on your merchandise, you may have to invest more money to have a climate-controlled unit.

Hopefully, you have found out it is legal and not too restrictive (if at all) to operate a business from your home. You have probably discovered that service businesses are generally allowed without much restriction, except perhaps for employees and client traffic. You may or may not be allowed to have a sign to advertise your business. We'll address the sign issue in Chapter 6, "A Corner Office or a Corner of the Dining Room?"

Some Horror Stories

If all this seems senseless to you—because, after all, it is your home you're using and you're not bothering anyone else—beware. Here are just a few of the horror stories about home-based business owners who didn't check the ordinances before starting their home-based businesses.

A couple in Frederick, Maryland, spent two years and over $20,000 fighting antiquated zoning ordinances after a neighbor turned them in. The neighbors stated that the increase in mail delivery trucks was endangering their children. The reality was, the neighbors were mad that they were not invited to the couple's fiftieth birthday party. The couple moved to another area even though the zoning ordinances were changed in their favor.

A woman in Los Angeles, California, had been designing costumes in her home for years when she was shut down. The person who turned her in claimed she was doing something illegal because of all the strangers coming to her house.

A couple in Fredricksburg, Virginia, was shut down for operating a home-based business when an anonymous caller complained about them. They had a graphic design business in the basement of a town house, with no client traffic. However, the ordinances prohibited any kind of business in the town houses, and they were not allowed a special exception due to the neighbor getting a group of other neighbors to come to the hearing and speak against the special exception.

These are just three of the many stories we have heard about or been involved with over the past 10 years. In each case, a neighbor's complaint brought government officials knocking on the door of the home-based business. Yes, it was illegal by zoning ordinance to be operating. You would think it would be a case of no harm, no foul. But for personal, emotional reasons, someone turned them in; and the officials are obliged to follow the law.

It's up to each potential and current home-based business owner to investigate, educate, and advocate for changes to antiquated zoning ordinances. The information in this chapter will help you do just that.

Chapter 3

KEEPING IT LEGAL

Dealing with Licenses, Taxes, and Organizational Forms

The government is your friend. Government officials believe strongly in the value of home-based businesses and want to do everything in their power to help you succeed.

And if you believe that, we've got some lovely swampland in Florida to sell you.

To a home-business owner, it can seem as if the government's sole purpose is to make your life difficult. The maze of regulations you have to navigate to secure the necessary licenses can be tremendously frustrating. And once your business is operating, the taxes you have to pay at the federal, state, and sometimes local level may be your biggest expense. In some localities, you have to pay business taxes even if you *lose* money.

But as difficult as complying with government regulations and tax policies may be, we still have to do it. The consequences for noncompliance can be severe, ranging from fines to jail time. And in this age of heightened ethical awareness, wouldn't you rather be proud that you're running your business the right way?

In this chapter we'll review some of the licenses you may need to start and operate your home-based business. Next, we'll discuss some of the taxes you'll have to deal with. And finally, we'll examine the different organizational forms your business might take.

Obviously, we can't provide specific details about the licensing and tax rules you personally will face. With 50 states and thousands of localities, each with its own regulations, it would be an impossible task. What we *can* do is give you some general guidelines about where to go and what to look for to get the specific answers you need. And we can wish you luck. You may need it.

LICENSES

While some localities are more home-business friendly than others, few—if any—are completely hands off. And there are legitimate reasons for that. Governments are charged with protecting people's safety and welfare and safeguarding us against con artists, cheats, and those who would harm others for personal gain. So local governments act as a watchdog, looking out for unscrupulous and unsafe businesses. To do their job, they need to know what businesses are operating in their jurisdictions.

Business License

The basic license required of nearly every business in every jurisdiction is a business license. Think of it as a birth certificate for your company. It confers legal operating status on your business and enables your local government to assess tax liabilities for it.

To apply for a business license, contact your city or county government. You can find the appropriate phone number in the white pages section of your local phone book. While the specific office varies from jurisdiction to jurisdiction, look for a business affairs office, a licenses division, or the clerk's office. You can also find information on your local government's Web site.

Home Occupation License

In most localities you need a separate permit to operate a business in your residence. These are typically called "home occupation licenses." Obtaining such a permit demonstrates that you are in compliance with local zoning ordinances and that you understand the local restrictions on home-based businesses (see Chapter 2).

If you need a home occupation license in your area, you can usually apply for it either at the same place you register for your business license or at your local zoning office.

Trade Name Registration

If you're going to use a name for your business other than your own, you need to register it as a "fictitious business name" or a "trade name" with your local government. Even if your name is *in* the business name, it still needs to be registered.

For example, "Pat Smith, CPA" does not need to be registered because it is the owner's legal name and title. It doesn't count as a trade name. However, "Pat Smith and Associates" *does* need to be registered. It is a company name that's separate and distinct from the owner's name.

The reason for requiring fictitious business names to be registered is to prevent multiple companies from operating under the same name in the same locality. If you try to register your trade name and find that some other company is already using it, you'll need to come up with another name. It's a good idea to brainstorm several potential business names before you try to register one; then, if your first choice is not available, you can immediately try your second choice.

You will most likely register your fictitious business name at the clerk's office of your county government, but it could also be the same office where you applied for your business license.

Note that the above information is applicable only if you intend to operate as a sole proprietorship or a partnership. If you plan to incorporate, you will go through a completely different name registration process with your state government.

Food Handling License

If you're going to be dealing with food that will be sold to the public, you'll need a food handling license. To get one, you have to prove that everyone involved in the food preparation understands safe food handling procedures. Your home must also pass one or more health inspections to ensure clean preparation conditions.

Food handling licenses are typically the responsibility of local health departments. So check there first for information on the application process.

Sales Tax License

Most states and localities impose sales taxes on various goods and services sold at retail. Business owners are responsible for collecting these taxes and remitting them to the appropriate taxing authorities. If you will be selling anything that is subject to sales tax, you'll need to obtain a sales tax license from your state government. You will then need to keep track of all sales and applicable taxes and remit sales taxes to your state and/or local government's taxation department on a regular basis.

If you purchase items at wholesale that will be resold at retail, be sure to provide a copy of your sales tax license to the wholesaler so you don't pay sales tax on your purchase. This is what is known as a "resale exemption." Sales taxes need to be paid only by the end consumer, not by any others in the process.

Employer Identification Number

Unless you are a sole proprietor with no employees, you must obtain an Employer Identification Number (EIN), also called a Federal Tax ID Number. This is a nine-digit number assigned to your business by the IRS for federal identification purposes. Think of it as a social security number for your company.

According to the IRS, you are required to obtain an EIN if you do one or more of the following:

• Form a C or S corporation or partnership
• Pay wages to one or more employees
• File pension or excise tax returns

If you will be operating as a sole proprietor with no employees, pension plans, or excise taxes, you can simply use your social security number as your Federal Tax ID Number.

To obtain an EIN, you'll need to fill out IRS Form SS-4, which you can request by phone or fax from the IRS or download from their Web site. For more information on how to determine whether you should obtain an EIN, check out the IRS publication *Understanding Your EIN*, also available by phone or on the Web.

TAXES

Unless you're an IRS agent or an accountant, it's hard to appreciate taxes. And the longer you operate your business, the harder taxes will be to appreciate. But then again, you're not *supposed* to love taxes. You're supposed to *pay* them.

With this in mind, your goal is to be aware of the various taxes to which you may be subject and to pay them in a timely manner. But there are steps you can take to minimize your tax burden. This is where a good accountant can be worth his or her weight in gold. An accountant can help you select the right business structure, set up effective record-keeping systems, find deductions, and take other actions that can save you a lot of money in taxes.

A good accountant is also necessary because of the number of tax jurisdictions and tax laws that may be applicable to your business. Not to mention the fact that tax laws change every year. Your accountant can keep you on the straight and narrow, preventing you from wasting money on fines and interest penalties.

As we discuss the major taxes you'll be subject to, keep in mind that this is only a general overview intended to provide some basic guidelines. Your accountant can work with you to help you understand the specific requirements of your state and locality.

There are four basic categories of taxes that you will be subject to. (There are also Four Horsemen of the Apocalypse. Coincidence?) Some are only levied by one level of government—local, state, or federal—while others may be applied by two or even all three. The four types of taxes are:

- Payroll taxes
- Self-employment tax
- Business property taxes
- Income taxes

Payroll Taxes

There are two different kinds of payroll (or employment) taxes: those paid by the employee and those paid by the employer. Either way, you have a responsibility in the taxation process.

If your business has employees, you are required to withhold several state and federal taxes from their paychecks and remit them periodically to the respective government agencies. The specific taxes you must withhold are the employee's state and federal income tax, social security tax (also known as FICA, for Federal Insurance Contributions Act), and Medicare tax.

In addition to withholding an employee's own taxes, you must pay several payroll taxes yourself. You are required to match your employee's FICA and Medicare taxes and to pay state and federal unemployment insurance taxes. These taxes cannot be deducted from your employee's earnings. For more detailed information, refer to IRS Publication 15, Circular E, *Employer's Tax Guide*.

Note that these tax requirements apply only to hourly or salaried employees. Independent contractors are responsible for their own taxes and you do not have to pay employment taxes on them. However, the IRS has very strict regulations governing the definition of an independent contractor to prevent companies from skirting tax laws via semantics. See Chapter 14, "Employees or Independent Contractors?" for more information on this issue.

Self-Employment Tax

Don't think for a second that just because you own your own business and you don't have any employees that you're going to get a break on social security taxes. Just the opposite. Whereas when you were an employee of someone else's company you paid half of the social security and Medicare taxes and your employer paid half, now that you work for yourself, you get to pay both halves! This is known as the "self-employment tax." Like income taxes, your self-employment tax is paid quarterly. For more information, read IRS Publication 533, *Self-Employment Tax.*

Business Property Taxes

Your local city or county may tax business personal property such as furniture, supplies, computers, and other office equipment. Unlike income taxes, business property taxes are not tied to the revenue or net income of your business. This means that if you operate at a loss, you will still have a tax liability. Check with your local government to find out if it levies business property taxes, and if so, what the procedures are for determining and paying them.

Income Taxes

If, heaven forbid, you somehow manage to turn a profit, you will, of course, have to pay taxes on that income at the federal, state, and possibly local level. Exactly how you file will depend on your type of business organization: sole proprietorship, partnership, or corporation. You'll need to consult with your accountant for specifics.

If, like most home-based entrepreneurs, you are not paying yourself a regular salary and withholding taxes from each check, you'll need to make estimated tax payments to both the federal and state governments on a quarterly basis.

Be aware that federal and state governments tax your business only on *net income*—that is, revenue minus expenses. Some localities also use this method, but others assess taxes on revenues instead—meaning your business could owe tax to your local government even if you suffer a loss for the year.

DEDUCTIONS
Business Expenses

Since your state and federal business income tax liability depends on your net income, it pays to keep good records of all your business expenses. In general, any expense that relates to your business is tax deductible as long as you have adequate proof. Get a copy of IRS Publication 583, *Starting a Business and Keeping Records,* and discuss expense strategy with your accountant.

Home Office

The single most important tax regulation for home-based business owners is the infamous home office deduction. Over the years, the definitions and applications of this deduction have been widened, narrowed, and widened again by Congress, the IRS, and the courts.

Rather than chance confusion by trying to summarize or paraphrase the latest version of the regulations, we've reprinted in the sections below the most salient details from the 2003 edition of IRS Publication 587, *Business Use of Your Home.*

Qualifying for a Home Office Deduction

To qualify to claim expenses for business use of your home, you must meet the following tests:

1. Your use of the business part of your home must be:
   a. Exclusive (however, see the section "Exceptions to Exclusive Use" later in this chapter)
   b. Regular
   c. For your trade or business

   AND

2. The business part of your home must be *one* of the following:
   a. Your principal place of business (defined later)
   b. A place where you meet or deal with patients, clients, or customers in the normal course of your trade or business, or
   c. A separate structure (not attached to your home) you use in connection with your trade or business

Exclusive Use

To qualify under the exclusive-use test, you must use a specific area of your home *only* for your trade or business. The area used for business can be a room or other separately identifiable space. The space does not need to be marked off by a permanent partition.

You do *not* meet the requirements of the exclusive-use test if you use the area in question both for business and for personal purposes. Here's an example:

You are an attorney and use a den in your home to write legal briefs and prepare clients' tax returns. Your family also uses the den for recreation.

The den is not used exclusively in your profession, so you cannot claim a business deduction for its use.

Exceptions to Exclusive Use

You do not have to meet the exclusive-use test if either of the following applies:

- You use part of your home for the storage of inventory or product samples (discussed below)
- You use part of your home as a day-care facility, which we'll discuss later

Storage of Inventory or Product Samples.   If you use part of your home for the storage of inventory or product samples, you can claim expenses for the business use of your home without meeting the exclusive-use test. However, you must meet all the following tests:

- You sell products at wholesale or retail as your trade or business.
- You keep the inventory or product samples in your home for use in your trade or business.
- Your home is the only fixed location of your trade or business.
- You use the storage space on a regular basis.
- The space you use is an identifiably separate space suitable for storage.

Here's an example:

Your home is the only fixed location of your business of selling mechanics' tools at retail. You regularly use half of your basement for storage of inventory and product samples. You sometimes use the area for personal purposes. The expenses for the storage space are deductible even though you do not use this part of your basement exclusively for business.

Regular Use

To qualify under the regular-use test, you must use a specific area of your home for business on a continuing basis. You do not meet the test if your business use of the area is only occasional or incidental, even if you do not use that area for any other purpose.

Trade or Business Use. To qualify under the trade- or business-use test, you must use part of your home in connection with a trade or business. If you use your home for a profit-seeking activity that is not a trade or business, you cannot take a deduction for its business use:

> You use part of your home exclusively and regularly to read financial periodicals and reports, clip bond coupons, and carry out similar activities related to your own investments. You do not make investments as a broker or dealer. So, your activities are not part of a trade or business and you cannot take a deduction for the business use of your home.

Principal Place of Business. You can have more than one business location, including your home, for a single trade or business. To qualify to deduct the expenses for the business use of your home under the principal place of business test, your home must be your principal place of business for that trade or business. To determine your principal place of business, you must consider all the facts and circumstances.

Your home office will qualify as your principal place of business for deducting expenses for its use if you meet the following requirements:

- You use it exclusively and regularly for administrative or management activities of your trade or business.
- You have no other fixed location where you conduct substantial administrative or management activities of your trade or business.

Administrative or Management Activities. Many activities are administrative or managerial in nature. Here are a few examples:

- Billing customers, clients, or patients
- Keeping books and records
- Ordering supplies
- Setting up appointments
- Forwarding orders or writing reports

Alternatively, if you use your home exclusively and regularly for your business, but your home office does not qualify as your principal place of business based on the previous rules, you determine your principal place of business based on the following factors:

- The relative importance of the activities performed at each location.
- If the relative importance factor does not determine your principal

place of business, you also can consider the time spent at each location.

If, after considering your business locations, your home cannot be identified as your principal place of business, you cannot deduct home office expenses. However, see "Place to Meet Patients, Clients, or Customers," below, for other ways to qualify to deduct home office expenses.

Administrative or Management Activities Performed at Other Locations.   The following activities performed by you or others will not disqualify your home office from being your principal place of business:

- You have others conduct your administrative or management activities at locations other than your home. For example, another company does your billing from its place of business.
- You conduct administrative or management activities at places that are not fixed locations of your business, such as in a car or a hotel room.
- You occasionally conduct minimal administrative or management activities at a fixed location outside your home.
- You conduct substantial nonadministrative or nonmanagement business activities at a fixed location outside your home. For example, you meet with or provide services to customers, clients, or patients at a fixed location of the business outside your home.
- You have suitable space to conduct administrative or management activities outside your home, but choose to use your home office for those activities instead.

More Than One Trade or Business
Whether your home office is the principal place of business must be determined separately for each trade or business activity. One home office may be the principal place of business for more than one activity. However, you will not meet the exclusive-use test for any activity unless each activity conducted in that office meets all the tests for the business use of the home deduction. Here's an example:

Tracy White is employed as a teacher. Her principal place of work is the school. She also has a mail order jewelry business. All her work in the jewelry business is done in her home office, and the office is used exclusively for that business. If she meets all the other tests, she can deduct expenses for business use of her home for the jewelry business.

If Tracy also uses the office for work related to her teaching, she would not meet the exclusive-use test for the jewelry business. As an employee, Tracy must meet the convenience-of-the-employer test to qualify for the deduction. She does not meet this test for her work as a teacher, so she cannot claim a deduction for the business use of her home for either activity.

Place to Meet Patients, Clients, or Customers

If you meet or deal with patients, clients, or customers in your home in the normal course of your business, even though you also carry on business at another location, you can deduct your expenses for the part of your home used exclusively and regularly for business if you meet the following tests:

- You physically meet with patients, clients, or customers on your premises.
- Their use of your home is substantial and integral to the conduct of your business.

Doctors, dentists, attorneys, and other professionals who maintain offices in their homes generally will meet this requirement.

Using your home for occasional meetings and telephone calls will not qualify you to deduct expenses for the business use of your home.

The part of your home you use exclusively and regularly to meet patients, clients, or customers does not have to be your principal place of business.

Authors' Note

The regulations governing the deductibility of a home office are still subject to change at any time. We recommend that you request the latest revision of Publication 587, *Business Use of Your Home*, from the IRS or download it from their Web site and review it with your accountant.

CHOOSING AN ORGANIZATIONAL FORM

One of your most important decisions is whether your business will be a sole proprietorship, a partnership, or some type of corporation. The organizational form your business takes affects its legal status and what you'll pay in taxes. This is another area in which a good accountant or attorney can be invaluable, because the variety of factors involved can make your decision extremely difficult. Here is a brief overview of the different types of organizational forms.

Sole Proprietorship

This is the simplest and least costly way of starting your business. You own all the assets and you are personally liable for any and all liabilities. In effect, you *are* the business. The business's income is reported as your income on your individual tax return.

The advantages to this approach are:

- Easiest and quickest way to get started
- Lowest start-up costs
- Minimal paperwork
- Maximum authority and freedom of action
- Simplest record keeping

There are some disadvantages, however:

- Unlimited liability
- Death, injury, or illness endanger the business
- Business finances can become easily mixed with personal

Partnership

If you're planning to go into business with someone else, a sole proprietorship is obviously not appropriate. A partnership might be. In a partnership, the business's assets are jointly owned by the individuals involved. Profits and losses are shared by the partners in a manner they decide ahead of time. Typically, each partner is personally liable for the company's liabilities. (Limited partnerships are an exception.) The partnership itself is not subject to income taxes. Instead, each partner reports their share of the firm's income on their own personal tax return and is taxed at their respective rates.

Advantages of a partnership include:

- More talents, skills, and expertise than going it alone
- Easier to get financing
- Profits and losses may be shared disproportionately
- Less complex and costly to start than a corporation
- Less paperwork and record keeping than a corporation

Disadvantages include:

- Personal liability for partner's actions
- Death, injury, or illness of one partner may endanger the business
- Clash of vision, values, personalities, or egos can destroy the company
- Hazy lines of authority and responsibility

Because of the above disadvantages, partnerships have the highest rate of business failure. To help ensure that yours is a success, craft a written partnership agreement, preferably with the help of your lawyer. The agreement should include the following:

1. Type of business
2. Amount of capital invested by each partner
3. Nonmonetary assets contributed by each partner
4. Compensation for each partner
5. Division of profits or losses
6. Ownership of intellectual property
7. Responsibilities and authority of each partner
8. Restrictions on authority and/or expenditures
9. Dispute resolution process
10. Provisions for admission or withdrawal of partners
11. Settlement in the event of death or incapacitation
12. Duration of partnership
13. Provisions for dissolving partnership
14. Distribution of company assets upon dissolution

Corporation

There are two types of corporations: C and S. A C corporation is the traditional corporate structure that all large and most midsized businesses use. An S corporation (so called because S is the subchapter of the law that created this type of legal entity) is a simplified, more limited structure that is frequently better suited for small businesses.

In either type of corporation, the company itself is a legal entity, distinct from the people who own it. The business owns its assets and is responsible for its liabilities. The owners of the company split profits based on the number of shares each owns in the company. The corporation must have a board of directors and at least three officers—a president, secretary, and treasurer, although one person may hold two or even all three positions.

The biggest difference between the two types of corporations is how they are taxed. A C corporation is a separate taxpayer, for which you must file corporate tax returns and pay corporate taxes on company profits. When you receive your share of the net profits (also known as dividends) you then pay personal income tax on that amount. This is known as *double taxation* because the same profits are taxed twice, first at the corporate level and then at the personal level.

The S corporation was created to solve this dilemma for small business owners. In an S corporation, profits are passed along directly to the stockholders, who declare them on their personal returns. This way, the profits are only taxed at the personal level.

There are other differences as well between the two types of corporations, which make it so important to get good guidance from a legal, business, and/or tax professional when you are choosing. With either type, though, here are some of the advantages of incorporating:

- Limited liability
- Continuity
- Ability to transfer shares
- Easier to raise capital
- Keeps business and personal affairs separate and distinct

Naturally, however, there are also some disadvantages:

- Most complex approach
- More paperwork
- Legal formalities
- Double taxation with a C corporation
- Highest start-up costs
- Less freedom

Limited Liability Company

There is one other form of business now being recognized by most states called a limited liability company or LLC. An LLC does just what is says—provides limited liability to the owner without a cumbersome corporation. Thus, an LLC gives the business owner the ease and simplicity of a sole proprietorship without the unlimited personal liability. For this reason, more and more home-based businesses are being formed as LLCs.

So which approach is right for you and your business? Take some time to think the issue through carefully and consult with one or more of the professionals we've recommended. The time and effort you invest in this decision will save you time, money, and headaches down the road.

Chapter 4
MAPPING OUT YOUR ROUTE TO SUCCESS
How to Write a Home-Based Business Plan

You've probably heard it before: "People don't plan to fail, they fail to plan." That's especially true for home-based business owners. Just because your business isn't going to be a huge multinational corporation (at least, not yet) doesn't mean you don't need a plan. You do. One characteristic that almost all failed home-based businesses share is that they didn't have a written business plan.

It's an understandable lapse. Most of us avoid writing a business plan for one or more significant reasons:

- It seems complicated and overwhelming.
- We have no idea how to do it.
- No one told us we needed one.
- We convinced ourselves we don't need one.
- We were too busy doing everything else related to starting up our business.

But while these are all good excuses, they are still just excuses. They won't help you when and if it's time to get financing or you have to make some strategic decisions. A well-written business plan will.

PURPOSE OF A BUSINESS PLAN

If you were going to drive from New York to San Francisco, you wouldn't just jump in the car and head out on the highway. If you did, there's a good chance you'd never make it, and even if you did, it would almost certainly be a rotten trip. To make the trip "successful," you'd want to figure out your goals, priorities, and budget.

Do you want to complete the trip as quickly as possible or do you want to take scenic routes? Would you rather stay in luxury hotels, midlevel hotels, or budget hotels? Or would you rather camp? How long will you drive each day? And if there's more than one of you, how often will you change drivers? How often and where will you stop to eat? How much money can you afford to spend on the whole trip? What will you do if you run out? What if the car breaks down? How will you adjust if you end up behind schedule? And what the heck are you going to do once you get to San Francisco?

You don't necessarily have to plan everything down to the last detail. And you can't anticipate everything. But the more you plan, the more you know what to expect and the better you can adjust to make sure you get to your destination without being too stressed to enjoy it.

The path to home-business success is much longer and much more complicated than a trip across the country. But like a trip, it should be as enjoyable as possible. That is, after all, one of the reasons you've chosen to start a home-based business—you want to enjoy the unique lifestyle that working at home affords. And the more you plan now, the more enjoyment you'll experience later.

COMPONENTS OF AN EFFECTIVE PLAN

There are several different approaches to writing a plan. Most involve the same basic components organized in different ways. Our favorite structure breaks down the business plan into eight distinct components:

1. Executive summary
2. Company description
3. Industry analysis
4. Marketing plan
5. Financial plan
6. Strategic analysis
7. Personal background
8. Personal and family plan

Let's examine each of these components.

Executive Summary

The executive summary is a brief overview of your business plan. Sort of the *Reader's Digest* condensed version. It quickly communicates the essentials of your plan to the reader, preferably in one or two pages. A loan officer or potential investor reads the summary and then, based on its strength and clarity, decides whether to bother reading the rest of your plan. So this first impression must be a strong one.

The executive summary should be the first part of your plan that you write, and the last part. What we mean by this is that you should write your summary first to get your basic ideas on paper. You can then expand on those ideas in each of the other sections of your plan. As you flesh out each section, you'll come up with more ideas, questions, and potential problems. Keep writing until you're satisfied. When your plan is more or less complete, turn your attention back to your summary. Rewrite, tweak, and edit it to make it stronger and clearer.

Company Description

The second part of your business plan is where you describe your company. Include as many salient details as possible, including:

- Company name and purpose
- Company history (if any)
- Legal structure—proprietorship, partnership, or corporation
- Products and services you will be selling
- Unique aspects of products or services
- Existing customers (if any)
- People who are involved in the company, and in what capacities
- Company resources
- Competitive strengths and weaknesses

Industry Analysis

Both you and your banker need to understand the potential and the risks involved in your industry. A growing industry with little competition means lots of opportunity. A stagnant or shrinking industry with lots of competition means much less opportunity. The industry analysis section of your plan should reflect the research you've done into the industry. Include:

- A description of the industry
- Market size
- Growth rate
- Key growth factors
- Product or service life cycle
- Industry average profit margins
- A listing of competitors
- A brief analysis of competitors' strengths and weaknesses

Marketing Plan

The first three parts of your business plan are fairly simple and straightforward. The fourth part will likely take you more time and effort, but the results will be well worth it. Most home-based entrepreneurs don't have a marketing plan, and as a result, their marketing message is ineffective, their marketing efforts go unnoticed, and their marketing dollars are wasted. And without good marketing, it's extremely hard to get new or even return customers.

Fortunately, you don't need an MBA in marketing to write a solid marketing plan. All you need to do is ask yourself six fundamental questions. The answers will form the basis of a powerful marketing plan that can make all the difference for your business.

1. What am I selling?

The answer to this question is not what it seems. You're not selling insurance, or vacation packages, or advertising opportunities, or Web design, or anything related to telecommunications. In fact, you're not *really* selling any product or service at all. What you're selling is the results you bring to your customers. The product or service is simply how the result is achieved.

The simple, ego-bursting fact is that prospects don't care who we are, what we do, or how we do it. All they really care about is how our product or service will impact them. What problems of theirs will we solve? How will we improve their lives?

For example, Don speaks on sales and marketing to companies and associations all over the world. But he's not selling speeches. He's selling higher sales and profits. No one really wants to buy a speech, but they *do* want higher sales and profits.

So ask yourself: What are the results that you deliver to your customers? Will their health be improved? Will they have more free time to spend with their families? Will they be safer and more secure? Or something else? Define the result and it becomes much easier to market your offering.

2. Who are my customers?

"Everyone" is the wrong answer. No company can market effectively to everybody, and lord knows you sure can't with *your* budget. And no matter how wonderful your product or service is, some people will want it more than others. These two factors mean that you have to target your marketing to your best prospects: the people who need or want you most.

So, define your best prospects. Business or consumer? What is their annual income (or revenue)? How old are they? Male or female? Married or single? Any kids? Rural, urban, or suburban? Industry? What do they do for fun? What do they read, watch, and listen to? The more you know about your customers, the better you can position your product or service to appeal to them, and the better your return on your marketing investment will be.

For example, Don is a young, single male living in Denver, Colorado. Bev is a married female with children and grandchildren who lives in rural Maryland. We have completely different needs, likes, values, and priorities. So a message that resonates with one of us will likely be ignored by the other. Which means if you're marketing to both of us, you're wasting at least some of your time, energy, and money. On the other hand, if you're marketing to just one of us, along with other people who fit the same demographic profile, you're going to get a lot more bang for your marketing buck.

Here are some consumer demographic criteria you can use to define your target market:

- Age
- Sex
- Race/ethnicity
- Education level
- Geographic area
- Urban/suburban/rural resident
- Housing type, i.e., detached house, town home, condominium, mobile home, etc.
- Homeowner or renter
- Marital/family status
- Family size

- Age of children
- Number of children
- Religion
- Height and weight
- Hobbies/interests
- Recreational activities
- Job status
- Profession
- Household income
- Disabilities
- Pet ownership

Some of these criteria can be further subcategorized. For instance, pet owners can be subdivided by number of pets or type of pet owned: dog, cat, fish, bird, etc.

If you're marketing to businesses, consider these demographic criteria:

- Industry or profession
- Geographic area
- Age of business
- Target market of the business
- Job title
- Workforce size
- Annual revenue
- Number of locations
- Business type, i.e., manufacturing, service, distribution, retail, restaurants, etc.

The more specifically you can define your target customer, the more effectively you can market to them, so use as many demographic characteristics as you can. For example, your target customer might be overweight single women under the age of 30 living in the Seattle metropolitan area. Or your target customer might be male retirees living in the southwestern United States with incomes between $100,000 and $500,000. Or your target customer might be Pennsylvania businesses with annual revenues under $1 million which have been in business less than one year. Or it could be female medical malpractice attorneys throughout the country.

This is not to say that these are the only people you will sell to. You may well have customers outside your target market. And you may have two or even three distinct target markets, each with its own unique characteristics.

But the more narrowly you can define your market, the more effectively you can craft a marketing message that resonates with them, and the more cost effectively you can present that message to them.

Remember, too, that repetition is crucial to marketing success. You have to get your message in front of your prospects numerous times before they buy from you. Which means you'll get far better results marketing to 1,000 targeted people ten times than marketing to 10,000 random people once.

3. Where are my customers?

Whoever your ideal prospects are, you'll find some of them everywhere. But what you want to know is where can you reach the greatest concentrations of them. That's where you will get the biggest bang for your marketing buck.

To find them, ask yourself—and them—questions like:

- Where are they located?
- What specialty publications are targeted at them?
- What do they read?
- Where do they congregate?
- What organizations do they belong to?
- What do they do for fun?
- What Web sites do they spend time at?

4. How many customers do I need?

The obvious answer to this question would seem to be: "As many as possible." But think again. Certainly, if you have too few customers, you can't stay in business. But if you have more customers than you can handle, they will be unhappy with you and let others know about it. Your reputation is the most valuable asset you have, and it is the hardest thing to repair.

So think carefully about the answer to this question. Figure out how many customers you need in order to cover your costs, pay yourself an acceptable income, and turn some kind of profit. Then determine how many customers you can adequately serve with your present resources. That way you can adjust your marketing to bring in enough customers without attracting too many.

5. Why do my customers need me?

The opposite of love is not hate, but indifference. And that's precisely what you'll face in the marketplace. Because the competition is so heavy in almost every industry in almost every part of the country, in order to convince your prospect to choose your business, you have to make the case to your prospect why they should choose you.

Yes, yes, we know you're the best. Your product is of the highest quality and you provide excellent customer service. But that's exactly what your competitors say too. So saying it yourself is meaningless.

Instead, what makes you *different* from your competition? What makes you *unique*? It's important to understand your USP (unique selling proposition). Are you cheaper, faster, more reliable? Is your product safer or easier to use? Are you more environmentally friendly? Is your product smaller, lighter, or available in more styles or colors? Can you customize to your client's needs? Are you a specialist in a sea of generalists? And above all: *Why are these differences beneficial to your customer?*

To be able to make a persuasive case to your prospects, you need to understand their buying motivations:

- What are their hopes, dreams, and desires?
- What are their fears and concerns?
- What gets them excited and what bores them?
- What are their priorities?
- What do they want more of and less of in their lives?
- What pressures are they under?
- What have their past buying experiences been like?

Understanding their motivations will enable you to create a marketing proposition that will be the underlying message in all your marketing efforts. And that will put you head and shoulders above most of your competition.

6. How will I reach my customers?

Once you've developed your primary marketing message, you have to figure out how you're going to get it in front of your prospects. Most home-based entrepreneurs do very little marketing because they don't understand it and don't know how to get their message out without spending a lot of money. (Which, like you, they don't have.)

To address this critical need, in Chapter 10, "Getting the World to Beat a Path to Your Door," we'll present more than 40 different marketing tactics for your consideration. All are low-cost or free, and they're all suitable for home-based businesses. As you read through all the different marketing ideas, note the ones that excite you the most and include them in your marketing plan.

Answering these six marketing-related questions will probably take you a considerable amount of time and effort. (Hey, we didn't say this was going to be easy.) It may help to talk with someone outside your business who can see things more dispassionately. Once you have some clear answers, your marketing plan will start to come into focus.

Financial Plan

Like your marketing plan, your financial plan will take some work, but it will pay you massive dividends. Too many home-based businesses start out underfunded and suffer because of it. The lack of available cash acts as a stranglehold on their business, preventing growth and often leading to bankruptcy.

Very few businesses turn a profit quickly. Depending on the type of business you'll be running and the start-up costs required, it could take you a couple of years or more before you become profitable. But even if it takes you less than a year to see profits, you still need enough cash to get you to that point. If you don't have enough money to pay the bills, you're in trouble.

So before you start your business, you've got to figure out how much money you'll need to pay your expenses until your business becomes self-sustaining. That's the amount of start-up capital you need. This requires some guesswork, since you can't accurately predict what your future sales and expenses will be. Which is why, when you do your planning, you should estimate your revenues conservatively and your expenses liberally.

Here's a step by step approach to calculating how much start-up capital you'll need:

1. Prepare a personal expense budget for one year.
2. Determine your current net worth.
3. Decide how much cash you can invest in your business.
4. Estimate the start-up costs for your business.
5. Estimate your first-year business expenses.
6. Estimate your three-year business expenses.
7. Estimate your first-year revenues.
8. Estimate your three-year revenues.
9. Determine your break-even point, accounting for your start-up costs.
10. Estimate your combined personal and business cash requirements for the period of time between your first day of business and your break-even point.

11. Determine how much you need to borrow by subtracting the amount of cash you can invest (item 3) from your combined cash requirements (item 10).

You don't need to include these calculations in your business plan, though if you're going to be seeking financing from others, you'll want to include your expected start-up costs, revenue, and expense estimates, and your anticipated break-even point.

Whether you'll be seeking outside financing or not, you want to include the actual amount of start-up capital you'll need. You also want to list exactly what the capital will be used for. Writing down all your anticipated expenses will help ensure that you don't overlook any. Include expenses such as:

- Your salary
- Salaries for other employees (if any, at this point)
- Rent (refer back to Chapter 3 for details on deducting rent costs for your home office)
- Utilities
- Inventory
- Office equipment
- Supplies
- Marketing
- Interest on borrowed funds
- Professional services
- Insurance
- Travel
- Postage

Now that you've explained to yourself and any potential lenders what your start-up capital will be used for, you want to address some other issues, including:

- Where you plan to obtain your start-up funding
- When you'll need it
- How long you'll need it for
- When you can start repaying it
- How quickly you can repay it
- What you'll do if your estimates are wrong and you need additional funds

It's a good idea to have an accountant or a financially savvy business consultant review your financial plan. He or she can point out areas where your estimates may be overly optimistic and remind you of issues you may have overlooked. Having a financial professional's seal of approval on your financial plan will also make it easier for you to get funding from a lending institution.

Strategic Analysis

In this section, you'll be planning your strategy and establishing management benchmarks. This provides two benefits. First, it gives you an opportunity to make your goals concrete. Goals that are measurable are more achievable. Second, it enables you to refer back to your plan at a later time to see if you're on track with your goals and assumptions. If you're not, it's better to discover this sooner than later so you can make adjustments.

Include in your strategic analysis:

- Company goals and objectives
- Plans for achieving goals
- Goal completion schedule
- Operating assumptions
- Key performance benchmarks

Personal Background

In a business plan for a larger company, you'd need a section that discusses the management team and the organizational hierarchy. Since the odds are good that the only person on your management team is you, this section can instead simply be a review of your personal background.

Think of it as being similar to a résumé. Any lending institution or investor is going to want to know what kind of person is behind this company and why they should believe that you're going to be successful. Focus on your experience, accomplishments, and what skills you bring to your company. And if there are going to be other people involved in a management-type capacity, be sure to include their biographical information as well.

Personal and Family Plan

As a home-based business owner, you need one additional component in your business plan that other kinds of companies don't—a personal and family plan. Running a business in the same house that you and your family live in presents special challenges that you need to address sooner rather than later. We'll discuss in detail the benefits and difficulties of working with family in Chapter 12, "Making It a Family Affair," but in this section we will review some of the issues you want to plan for to make sure that your business and your family can peacefully coexist.

What do you expect of your spouse or partner in relation to your business? What can your spouse expect from you? And what about your kids? A business in the home can bring a family closer together or it can place a tremendous strain on family relationships. (It can even do both.)

Fortunately, discussing your intentions and expectations ahead of time can prevent misunderstandings and tensions. Sit down with your spouse, partner, and/or children and work out issues such as:

• Work time vs. family time
• Personal and professional boundaries
• Business vs. family priorities
• Business vs. family finances
• Household chores
• Involving family members in the business

If you can agree on these issues as a couple or as a family, people will be much more likely to abide by the agreed-upon decisions than if you simply make a decree about the way things are going to be. When you show your family that you respect their needs, opinions, and feelings, they will be much more likely to respect your personal needs and your business needs.

If you are single and have no kids, you still need a personal plan. Working at home by and for yourself can present a variety of new challenges. With your office only a few steps away from everything else in your house, it's very easy for your personal time and your business time to get mixed together. It's also easy for one part of your life to eclipse the other. And you may experience feelings of isolation that will require you to plan time outside your office. So you need to plan now for how you're going to manage your time and balance your business and personal life.

You don't need to include this last section of your business plan in the version you show to accountants, lawyers, and bankers. This section is just for you and your family.

A FEW RANDOM THOUGHTS ABOUT BUSINESS PLANS

After you finish the first draft of your business plan, show it to as many people as possible, in as many different fields of expertise as possible, for feedback. Ideally, you should show it to an attorney, an accountant, a banker, and a small business consultant. If you have a business mentor, by all means show it to him or her. The more professional feedback you get, the stronger your plan will be, and the greater the chances that your business will succeed.

Be clear in your explanations. Don't leave out crucial steps or assume you'll "figure it out when you get there." If you can't figure out now how you'll get from point A to point B, stop and hold everything until you come up with an answer.

Include backup plans throughout your business plan. A business plan that assumes everything will happen just as you expect is doomed to failure. Anticipating problems and setbacks shows others that you've thought ahead. It will also make those problems easier to deal with if they actually occur.

Quantity does not equal quality. Your plan, while thorough, should be succinct. A loan officer once told us he had seen great business plans that were 50 pages and great plans that were 5 pages.

First impressions are lasting impressions. Spelling errors, poor grammar and punctuation, numbers that don't add up, and other minor flaws can collectively ruin an otherwise great plan. Lenders will judge your plan in part on how it looks. If it's sloppy, they will assume your logic, planning skills, and business acumen are sloppy too. Have your business plan proofread by a professional editor or proofreader if you'll need it to secure financing. Even if you won't need it for that, have it proofread by two or three people anyway. It's good to get into that habit early.

Once you get your business started, don't just throw your business plan in a folder and file it away forever. Review it at least once a quarter. Check your assumptions, your key performance benchmarks, and your revenue and expense estimates. Reviewing and updating your plan regularly will help you stay on track and make needed adjustments. You'll not only be on the path to home-business success, you'll be in the fast lane.

Chapter 5

PIGGY BANKS AND MEGABANKS

Options for Financing Your Business

If you're independently wealthy, you can skip this chapter. If you're not, this chapter will give you ideas for getting the money you need to start and run your business. And you're going to need it. Because whatever kind of business you're in, it requires money to get started, to survive and to grow.

Just to open for business, you'll need office equipment, stationery, supplies, and possibly inventory. Then as you go, you'll have regular expenses such as insurance, utilities, services, taxes, and perhaps labor. And at some point, *you'd* probably like to be paid.

Fortunately, running your business from home means that some of your expenses are lower than they would otherwise be. You don't have to pay additional rent, the increase in usage of your utilities is minimal, and you may be able to cajole friends or family members into providing at least some labor at little or no cost.

Nonetheless, your business will need capital to survive and grow. Keep in mind that most businesses aren't profitable for several years. To get you through that time, you need enough capital to supplement your anticipated business revenues, as we discussed in the previous chapter. You also need to figure out what personal money you'll need and where that will come from. If you are the sole income provider or your income is imperative to the household, you'll have to take this into account now.

There are a variety of ways for you to raise the capital you need to start your business and keep it running until it turns profitable. None of them is perfect, of course, and no one approach is inherently better than the others. Each has its own advantages and disadvantages. We will explore each of the options available to you, starting with the least complicated and lowest risk. Bear in mind that the right approach for you might be a combination of tactics.

PERSONAL SAVINGS

Unquestionably, the easiest, fastest, most risk-free way to finance your home business is to do it yourself. If you have enough money saved up to provide your business with the start-up and operating capital it needs, this is definitely the way to go.

Using your personal savings means you don't have to go through the long, tedious process of arranging financing through a lender. It also means you don't have to be accountable to anyone but yourself, so you retain complete control. You don't have to pay interest on a loan, and that will save your business money. And you don't have to make regular loan payments, which frees up your cash flow.

But you may not have enough money in savings to finance your business. Or maybe that money is earmarked for your children's education or to pay for an elderly relative's living expenses or something else that's important to you and your family. In that case, you'll need to explore other ways of raising cash.

SELLING ASSETS

Another way to "do it yourself" is to sell personal assets and use the proceeds to fund your business. You may find a considerable amount of money tied up in assets you don't really need, wouldn't mind parting with, or that are less important to you than starting your own business. Think about what kinds of assets you could liquidate:

- An extra car
- Motorcycle
- Boat
- Jewelry
- Baseball cards, comic books, stamps, coins, or other collectibles
- Artwork
- Stocks and/or bonds
- Antiques
- Furniture

- Vacation home
- Rental property

If your children have left the house, you may even want to consider selling your current home, buying a less expensive one, and putting the difference into your business.

With the advent of eBay and other online auctions, selling unwanted assets is easier than ever before. If you've never used an online auction before, there are several books that will walk you through the entire process and even give you tips on maximizing your selling price.

WORKING ANOTHER JOB

There's no rule that says you must start your business full-time and devote all your time and energy solely to it. Many people start their businesses part-time while working full- or part-time at another job. It's a simple, straightforward approach that keeps you free of debt.

The benefit is that it lowers your risk. If your business fails, you lose only what you yourself have invested in it. You also are guaranteed an income while getting your new business off the ground.

The downside is that the more time you spend working for someone else, the less time you have to work for yourself. This creates one or both of two problems. Problem one is that the less time you have to devote to your business, the slower it will grow. Problem two is that between your job and your business, you will have even less time to spend with your family.

If you have a relatively high-paying job that allows you flexible hours, it may be to your advantage to keep it during your early start-up phase until you absolutely need to devote more time to your business. Or if you can find a part-time job you enjoy doing, one that is not stressful or that gives you time to read or plan during your work hours, it may be worth taking even if it's low-paying.

But if your business requires a lot of time and energy or you're trying to achieve more balance between your working life and your family life, you'll probably be better off focusing on your business than trying to split your time and attention.

CREDIT CARDS

More than 50 percent of home-based business owners use personal credit cards as their primary business financing. And it's easy to see why. The ease and flexibility of credit cards make them a convenient choice.

First, credit cards are easy to get. You probably have several already. And you probably receive offers for more almost every week. With the tremendous competition among financial institutions to issue credit cards, you can apply for, and receive, several more cards if your credit history is decent. All you have to do is fill out a simple form. No lengthy applications, no business plans, no loan officers.

The second big attraction of credit cards is that they're flexible. Just because you have a $10,000 limit on a card doesn't mean you have to use it (and pay interest on it) all at once. You can take smaller cash advances as you need them or use your cards to pay for various expenses as you go. You also have flexibility when it comes to paying off your cards. Since the minimum payments are usually very low, you can make smaller payments when cash is tight and larger payments when you're more flush.

However, you pay a price for this convenience. Credit cards are among the most expensive forms of financing available. While many cards offer low introductory rates, the interest can soar over 20 percent after the promotional period. And even if the card charges a more reasonable 10 percent or so on purchases, cash advances can remain twice as expensive.

The key to using credit cards effectively is to employ several important money management strategies:

- Look for cards with low rates that last beyond the introductory period.
- Look for no-annual-fee cards.
- Use your lowest interest cards first.
- Pay back your highest interest cards first.
- Transfer balances from one card to another when they offer you promotional "balance transfer" deals at low rates.
- Watch for specials when you can get cash without a cash advance fee.

FRIENDS AND FAMILY

Got a rich aunt? Or is a friend of yours looking for a good place to invest some excess cash? There are a number of advantages to borrowing money from friends and family:

- You can get lower interest rates than from a bank.
- You can get more lenient terms.
- You can wait longer before paying the money back.
- It can be easier to get more money if you need it.

- If you have a setback, your friends and family will be more understanding.
- If you miss a payment or are late, it won't hurt your credit rating.
- You don't have to risk your house or any other form of collateral.

Of course there are also a few disadvantages:

- Being in debt to your friends or family can make you feel awkward.
- Being late or missing payments can put a huge strain on the relationship.
- If your business fails, everyone knows where you live.
- Your family or friends may want to tell you how to run the business they've just invested in.

Because friendships and family relationships are so important, it pays to think twice about doing anything that might potentially put them in jeopardy. If these disadvantages concern you, it may be best to look at all your other options first.

Here are some guidelines to making it work:

- Never ask for money from somebody who can't afford to lose it.
- Don't take a rejection personally. (If you think you'll have a problem with this, don't even ask.)
- Let your family member or friend know that you don't want them to feel obligated and you won't be hurt if they say no.
- Don't pressure anyone.
- Agree on an interest rate and a repayment plan. (The rate should be fixed and lower than what a bank would charge you.)
- Agree on what will happen if you run into a problem
- Allow your friend or family member to check on your business periodically, and make financial statements available to them.
- Write everything down and make sure all people involved have a copy of the agreement.

FACTORING

If you've already gotten some clients but they haven't paid you as yet, consider factoring to get some cash flow. Let's say you've got $10,000 in receivables (money you're expecting to receive from clients). The trouble is, you're not going to get that money for 30 to 60 days and you've got bills to pay *now*.

There are finance companies that will purchase your receivables, paying you cash immediately for them. This process is called "factoring." While it's fast, flexible, and convenient, it's also expensive. Factoring companies typically only pay about 70 to 80 cents on the dollar, depending on the age of the receivables. So your finance charges can be enormous.

Why would someone pay such enormous costs? For one thing, factoring keeps your other lines of credit clear. If you run into a crunch and don't have any receivables, you'll need that other credit. Or maybe your new business doesn't have enough credit and you don't want to mix your personal credit with your business accounts. Also, factoring can save you a lot of time and effort. Once you've sold the receivables to the finance company, collecting them is their job. And if your customer never pays, it's the factoring company that takes the loss.

BANK LOANS

Here's an important secret to understand: Banks *want* to make loans. They *need* to make loans. Lending money is how banks make most of their profit. The fees we pay for our checking accounts and other services are small change for a bank. If they're not making loans, they're not making money.

So banks want to lend money. The key is to make them want to lend money to *you*. To do that, you have to persuade them that you are a low-risk investment. Banks are pretty risk averse. Their profit margin on loans is fairly small, so they can't afford many defaults. The more you can instill confidence in your ability to repay the loan, the more likely you are to get it.

In evaluating your loan-worthiness, most lenders use the six "Cs" of credit:

- Character
- Capacity
- Capital
- Collateral
- Coverage
- Circumstances

So what exactly do these six Cs mean? How do they affect your ability to secure a loan? And how can you make sure your Cs are as strong as they can be? Let's take a quick look at each one individually.

Character

What kind of person are you? Specifically, are you the kind of person who can be trusted to pay back what you borrow? This is the primary question your credit report answers. Lenders examine your credit history to determine how you manage your debts. Details that lenders look for include:

- Types of credit you've had
- Size of the debts you've carried
- Timeliness of your payments
- How quickly you've repaid loans
- Whether you've ever defaulted or declared bankruptcy

Because your credit history is such a big factor in your loan evaluation, you want to make sure that it is completely accurate. Odds are, it isn't. By some estimates, as many as 80 percent of all credit reports contain errors. And just one error can sink your application.

So contact one of the "Big Three" credit bureaus to request a copy of your credit report, and check it carefully before you begin the loan application process. You may be shocked by what you find. Once, when Don was checking his credit report, he discovered several accounts belonging to his grandfather (who shares the same first name) on his record.

Notify the bureau you received the report from of any errors you find, and follow up to make sure they get corrected. In theory, any credit bureau you report errors to is supposed to contact the other two and share the information, but it never hurts to double-check yourself.

To get a copy of your credit report, contact any of these companies:

- Equifax: 800-525-6285
- Experian (formerly TRW): 888-397-3742
- Trans Union: 800-680-7289

Capacity

The term *capacity* refers to your financial ability to repay what you're asking to borrow. Your capacity is based on several factors:

- Your projected business revenues
- Alternative personal income (from a full- or part-time job, a spouse's job, an annuity, etc.)

- Personal and family expenses
- Existing debt load from credit cards, mortgage, car loans, student loans, etc.
- The size and terms of the loan you're applying for

What a lender is concerned with is your debt-to-income ratio. In other words, how much does it cost you to service your debt and other expenses versus how much are you bringing in each month. The lower your debt-to-income ratio, the higher your capacity—and the better credit risk you are.

Lenders are also concerned about how viable your business is. For this reason, you should include your business plan with your loan application. If your business is already up and running, include a current balance sheet and recent income—also called "profit and loss" or "P&L"—statements. Be aware that many banks are reluctant to finance a home-based business unless you have some prior business experience.

Capital

A lending institution would typically rather not be the only one risking money in your home-based business. When you put up some of your own cash in your venture, you demonstrate that you believe strongly in what you're doing. The more of your own money you're committing to the business, the more confidence the bank has in you and the more likely you are to get the loan.

By contrast, if you're asking the bank to supply all the capital you need, and you aren't willing to risk any of your own money, it sends up a huge red flag. If you're not willing to do whatever it takes to finance your business, the lender will believe (and rightly so) that you won't be willing to do whatever it takes in other areas. And that's a surefire recipe for business failure.

Collateral

Bankers worry a lot. And one of the things they worry most about is what happens if someone defaults on a loan. That's where collateral comes in. Collateral is an asset that you put up against the value of the loan. It becomes the property of the lender in the event that you default.

Contrary to what many people believe, banks don't actually relish seizing your property and selling it. The process costs them a lot, so their return is a lot less than if the loan were simply repaid in the first place. But unless the amount of the loan is very small, most banks will insist on some form of collateral because it's their protection of last resort. And unless you have some business assets already, you will be asked to provide personal assets as collateral.

Coverage

What happens if there's a fire in your house? Or a flood? Or what if you get sued by a customer? Or what if something else goes wrong? Lenders, through experience, are among the most fervent believers in Murphy's Law: Anything that can go wrong, will go wrong.

To minimize the risks, your lender will want to see that you have insurance coverage. *Lots* of insurance coverage. The more types of insurance coverage you have—both personal and business—and the greater the amount you're insured for, the better your chances of landing financing. It will help you to talk with your loan officer as early in the process as possible to learn what kinds of coverage their bank likes to see. Refer to Chapter 6 for information on home-based business insurance needs.

Circumstances

Even if your other five Cs are not as strong as they could be, you're not doomed. Most lenders also consider intangibles, which while not measurable, can still be important. Your individual circumstances and the bank's particular circumstances can tilt things in your favor.

Here are some factors that can be to your advantage:

- You have a strong, well-thought-out business plan that has been reviewed by a lawyer, accountant, and/or a business consultant.
- You've taken one or more classes in business or entrepreneurship.
- You're getting counseling from your local Small Business Development Center.
- You have experience in sales, marketing, and/or management.
- Your business already has customers.
- You've just landed a big contract with a new client.
- You've got letters of reference testifying to your character.
- You have letters from other (ideally prominent) business owners endorsing your idea.
- You have a letter of support from a business mentor.
- You have multiple accounts at the bank.
- You have had an account at the bank for a long time.
- You know the bank manager or chief loan officer personally.
- You have successfully borrowed and repaid money from the bank before.

- You are an active member of your community.
- You are a friendly, upbeat, confident person.

Here are some possible bank circumstances that can work in your favor:

- The lending institution is small and caters specifically to small businesses.
- The lending institution is large and can afford greater risk.
- The bank has a surplus of cash and needs to make more loans.
- The bank is trying to improve its outreach to a particular geographic area, gender, or race.
- The bank is new in the area and trying to acquire local customers as quickly as possible.

The fact that your business is going to be home-based is a circumstance that can work for you or against you. Since your start-up costs are lower than other business, you need less money, making you a smaller risk. Because your operating expenses will be lower than comparable businesses, you have a better chance of succeeding, again reducing the level of risk.

Your home-based status can be an obstacle, however, if your bank officer is unaware of the success and growth in the home-based sector and as a result still has an image of home-based businesses as little more than glorified hobbies. If your loan officer or bank manager believes that your business is less serious and less viable than other businesses, share with them some of the facts about home-based businesses from our introduction. Make the case to them that your business is not merely just as viable as any other, but in point of fact is *more* viable because of your unique home-based advantages.

IF AT FIRST YOU DON'T SUCCEED . . .

When pursuing bank financing, it's critical to be persistent. You may very well be turned down by the first lending institution you approach. You may just as likely be turned down by the second. And the third. We've heard of home-based entrepreneurs who were turned down by more than 20 banks before finally succeeding.

So stay positive and focused. If a lender turns you down, ask for a detailed explanation. If it has something to do with you, your plan, or your application, and it's correctable, make the changes and return. If it's not something fixable, or if the reason has more to do with the bank than with you, ask the lender for referrals to other banks that might be a better fit for you. Above all, be patient and don't give up.

SBA LOAN PROGRAMS

The United States Small Business Administration (SBA) is charged with supporting the growth of small businesses throughout the country. One of their most important efforts is assisting small businesses in getting financing.

Contrary to popular belief, the SBA doesn't actually make loans to businesses. Instead, it provides guaranties to lenders, and it provides counseling and prequalification services to business owners seeking funding.

While the SBA has a wide variety of lending programs, we've focused here on the ones most appropriate for home-based businesses. (Special thanks to the SBA for providing detailed information on each of their programs.)

Prequalification Loan Program

You know all those credit card offers you get saying you're "preapproved" for a new card? This program is sort of the SBA's version of that. It allows you to have your loan application analyzed, strengthened, and endorsed by the agency to make it easier for you to get your loan request approved. The program focuses on your character, credit, and experience more than your assets, making it ideal for an entrepreneur who doesn't have much in the way of cash or collateral.

Here's more information, courtesy of the Small Business Administration:

The Prequalification Loan Program uses intermediary organizations to assist prospective borrowers in developing viable loan application packages and securing loans. This program targets low-income borrowers, disabled business owners, new and emerging businesses, veterans, exporters, rural and specialized industries.

The job of the intermediary is to work with the applicant to make sure the business plan is complete and that the application is both eligible and has credit merit. If the intermediary is satisfied that the application has a chance for approval, it will send it to the SBA for processing. To find out whether there is a prequalification intermediary operating in your area, contact your local SBA office. *Note:* Small Business Development Centers serving as intermediaries do not charge a fee for loan packaging. For-profit organizations will charge a fee.

Once the loan package is assembled, it is submitted to the SBA for expedited consideration. SBA conducts a thorough analysis of the case, using the same time frame and degree of analysis that it uses when processing requests under the regular method of delivery process.

If SBA decides the application is eligible and has sufficient credit merit to warrant approval, it will issue a commitment letter on behalf of the applicant. The commitment letter or prequalification letter indicates SBA's willingness to guaranty a loan made by a lender under certain terms and conditions. The intermediary then helps the borrower locate a lender offering the most competitive rates. The applicant then takes the letter and its application documents to a lender for a decision.

Basic 7(a) Loan Program

The most commonly used and most flexible SBA program is known as the 7(a) Loan Program. It is designed for small businesses that, while seemingly qualified, have had difficulty obtaining a loan through normal sources.

The following information is courtesy of the Small Business Administration:

7(a) loans are the most basic and most used type loan of SBA's business loan programs. Its name comes from section 7(a) of the Small Business Act, which authorizes the Agency to provide business loans to American small businesses.

All 7(a) loans are provided by lenders, who are called participants because they participate with SBA in the 7(a) program. Not all lenders choose to participate, but most American banks do. There are also some nonbank lenders who participate with SBA in the 7(a) program, which expands the availability of lenders making loans under SBA guidelines.

7(a) loans are only available on a guaranty basis. This means they are provided by lenders who choose to structure their own loans by SBA's requirements and who apply and receive a guaranty from SBA on a portion of this loan. The SBA does not fully guaranty 7(a) loans. The lender and SBA share the risk that a borrower will not be able to repay the loan in full. The guaranty is a guaranty against payment default. It does not cover imprudent decisions by the lender or misrepresentation by the borrower.

Under the guaranty concept, commercial lenders make and administer the loans. The business applies to a lender for their financing. The lender decides if they will make the loan internally or if the application has some weaknesses which, in their opinion, will require an SBA guaranty if the loan is to be made. The guaranty which SBA provides is only available to the lender. It assures the lender that in the event the borrower does not repay their obligation and a payment default occurs, the Government will reimburse the lender for its loss, up to the percentage of SBA's guaranty. Under this program, the borrower remains obligated for the full amount due.

A key concept of the 7(a) guaranty loan program is that the loan actually comes from a commercial lender, not the Government. If the lender is not willing to provide the loan, even if they may be able to get an SBA guaranty, the Agency cannot force the lender to change their mind. Neither can SBA make the loan by itself, because the Agency does not have any money to lend. Therefore it is paramount that all applicants positively approach the lender for a loan, and that they know the lender's criteria and requirements as well as those of the SBA. In order to obtain positive consideration for an SBA supported loan, the applicant must be both eligible and creditworthy.

In order to get a 7(a) loan, the applicant must first be eligible. Repayment ability from the cash flow of the business is a primary consideration in the SBA loan decision process, but good character, management capability, collateral, and owner's equity contribution are also important considerations. All owners of 20 percent or more are required to personally guarantee SBA loans.

All applicants must be eligible to be considered for a 7(a) loan. The eligibility requirements are designed to be as broad as possible in order that this lending program can accommodate the most diverse variety of small business financing needs. All businesses that are considered for financing under SBA's 7(a) loan program must: meet SBA size standards, be for-profit, not already have the internal resources (business or personal) to provide the financing, and be able to demonstrate repayment. Certain variations of SBA's 7(a) loan program may also require additional eligibility criteria.

SBA must determine if the principals of each applicant firm have historically shown the willingness and ability to pay their debts and whether they abided by the laws of their community. The Agency must know if there are any factors which impact on these issues. Therefore, a "Statement of Personal History" is obtained from each principal.

To offset the costs of the SBA's loan programs to the taxpayer, the Agency charges lenders a guaranty and a servicing fee for each loan approved. These fees can be passed on to the borrower once they have been paid by the lender. The amount of the fees are determined by the amount of the loan guaranty.

Micro-Loan Program

As a general rule, lending institutions would much rather make large loans than small ones. Because a bank incurs roughly the same costs processing and servicing a loan regardless of the size, it makes more profit on a larger loan than a smaller one.

This fact can make it difficult for home-based entrepreneurs who don't need very much start-up capital to procure financing. In response, the SBA created a program to spur the availability of so-called "micro-loans."

According to the SBA: "The Micro-Loan Program provides very small loans to start-up, newly established, or growing small business concerns. Under this program, SBA makes funds available to nonprofit community-based lenders (intermediaries) which, in turn, make loans to eligible borrowers in amounts up to a maximum of $35,000. The average loan size is about $10,500. Applications are submitted to the local intermediary and all credit decisions are made on the local level."

Small Office/Home Office Loan Initiative

While the SBA Micro-Loan Program is one solution to the challenge of securing small loan amounts, it's not a perfect one for home-based entrepreneurs. That's because the Micro-Loan Program uses "nonprofit community based lenders" rather than banks. This is a disadvantage for home-business owners, because for us, a relationship with a banking institution is extremely valuable.

In an effort to provide an alternative that would include local banks, the SBA Washington Metropolitan Area District Office consulted with Bev and developed the Small Office/Home Office (SOHO) Loan Initiative. Under this program, the SBA district office works with local banks to create a streamlined process with minimal paperwork for small businesses seeking loans between $5,000 and $15,000. Loan approval is based primarily on:

1. Personal credit history
2. Length of home ownership or rental (which shows stability)
3. Business/industry type
4. Average monthly sales or estimated monthly sales
5. Length of time in business
6. Total liquid assets (which must be less than $100,000)

This experiment has proven so successful in the Washington, D.C., area that it is being adopted in other parts of the country. To find out if the SOHO Loan Initiative is available in your area, contact your local SBA district office.

OTHER SBA RESOURCES

The Small Business Administration provides a wealth of useful information and services for entrepreneurs available free of charge through their Web site and through local Small Business Development Centers (SBDCs). You can find information on business laws, local regulatory requirements, importing and exporting, patents and trademarks, and many other topics. Services offered include training, counseling, disaster assistance, an online library, and more. To learn about all the SBA has to offer, or to find an SBDC near you, call them at 1-800-U-ASK-SBA or visit their Web site at www.sba.gov.

Chapter 6

A CORNER OFFICE OR A CORNER OF THE DINING ROOM?

Setting Up Your Home Office Space

There are advantages and disadvantages to living and working under the same roof. Where you set up the office will have a tremendous impact on your ability to concentrate on work. It can also impact your personal life and that of anyone else in the household. Some common areas for a home office space include:

- Spare bedroom
- Basement space
- Dining room table
- Library or formal living room

Some other spaces to consider if none of the above work for you:

- Sunroom
- Large closet
- Under a stairwell
- Attic
- End of a long hallway

Consider the following when deciding on the space you'll use for your home office.

- Client traffic
- Meeting space

- Storage
- Equipment
- Lighting
- Electrical service
- Family traffic patterns
- Noise levels

If you've already spoken with other members of the household about the impact of a home-based business on daily life in your house, you're ahead of the game. Let's look at the other issues.

CLIENT TRAFFIC

One of the first things to consider when determining where your office will be located is whether you will have clients coming to your home office.

If you anticipate client traffic, does your local zoning allow client traffic to your home-based business? If the answer is yes, begin looking at an area or room closest to the door your clients will enter. Is this a room others in the house normally use for daily activity? Is there somewhere else for them to go? Is the room conducive to meeting with clients? How will clients perceive the space—as an office or as someone's living space? Some clients may be uncomfortable conducting business in personal space.

Some zoning ordinances allow a small sign to be placed on the property for the business. Others don't allow any outward sign of a business being operated from the home. If possible, consider a small sign placed where clients will see it when approaching your property. The sign may simply say "Office" or display your business name. A sign near the door your clients are to use is helpful in directing client traffic to that door rather than the family door. In Bev's case, family and friends regularly used the carport entrance to the house and clients came to the front door. If a client inadvertently came through to the carport door, it was uncomfortable for everyone, since this was the personal or family area of the house.

The See, Hear, and Smell Principle

After visiting with a fellow home-based business owner a number of years ago, Bev developed the "See, Hear, and Smell Principle" for home-based businesses with client traffic. The sights, smells, and sounds of your house become so familiar you probably don't notice them. However, someone else may immediately pick up on the odor of what you had for dinner, whether you've changed the cat's litter box lately, where you and the family throw your coats, and what music or TV shows your family likes.

Although there have been jokes and even TV commercials about the sounds of pets in the background of a business call, be aware that people with allergies or a fear of dogs will be reluctant to come to your office a second time if their first experience with your pets is a negative one.

Generally, these issues don't have to be considered when operating your business in commercial space. They do have to be considered when you have a home-based business. Ask a trusted friend or your worst critic to act as a client coming to your home-based business. Ask them what they see, hear, and smell, and ask them to be as specific as they can without getting nitpicky. Take measures to reduce these issues to a minimum whenever and wherever possible.

Here are some things you can do:

- Ask the family/roommate's cooperation in cleaning up on a regular basis.
- Do a quick perusal of the client entrance area before starting work.
- Turn off the television.
- Bake bread or cookies (leaves a great aroma).
- Simmer spices in a Crock-Pot or potpourri simmer pot.
- Use plug-in air fresheners.

Be careful of spraying air fresheners or burning candles. Some people are highly allergic to them. Burning candles can also be forgotten during a client meeting and start a fire.

MEETING SPACE

It may not always be possible to meet with clients in your office space. For instance, if your office is in a spare bedroom on the upper floor, don't make clients walk through your personal space. Look for another area near the client entrance that could double as an alternative client meeting space. A lot of houses have a formal living room and a family room. Most people don't use the formal living room on a regular basis. This might be a good place to meet with clients in the home.

Bev was fortunate in her first home-based business to have a library to the left of the front foyer and a formal living room on the right. The rest of the house was situated in such a way that clients could not see any other rooms. There was also a powder room off the foyer that was convenient for clients.

The office was big enough for one or two clients to be seated comfortably, and she set up an old typing stand with a coffeepot and condiments so she didn't have to disappear into "personal" space in order to offer amenities.

In her situation, she also needed enough space to hold larger meetings regularly. Because her family did not use the formal living room except on rare occasions, she bought a conference table for the living room and moved personal objects to personal space.

Alternative Meeting Spaces

Not everyone wants or is able to have clients come to their home office. You do have alternatives for meeting with clients. Consider these options:

- Meet at your client's office.
- Meet in a hotel lobby.
- Meet at a restaurant.
- Meet at a coffee shop.
- Rent space in an executive office suite (look under "Office Rental" in your local yellow pages or check the resources list at the back of this book).

In addition, check with your local Chamber of Commerce. Some Chambers offer extra rooms for members to hold meetings either free or for a small fee. Wherever you meet with your clients, make the location convenient for them.

OFFICE OPTIONS

A Separate Room

Having a separate room for your office is ideal. Some of the advantages are:

- It's easier to concentrate on work and block out your personal life for a period of time.
- A door you can close makes it easier to leave work and to transition to personal life.
- A door can also be an appropriate barrier to family interruptions.

Basement offices can be damp and gloomy or light and airy. If there is a separate outside entrance that isn't difficult to get to, this might be a good place for your office. A friend of ours has a beautiful office in his basement, very professional-looking on the inside, but it's difficult to walk the sloping stone path around the side of the house that leads under his deck to the double glass doors to his office. There is no doorbell, and it can be very uncomfortable to just open the door and walk in. Some different landscaping and a sign on the door would be helpful.

On the positive side, our friend has an employee and there is plenty of space for her desk, supplies, reference books, and other business paraphernalia, as well as a bathroom nearby. He can also lock the door to the upstairs—the personal area of his house.

Spare Bedrooms

Others have used a spare bedroom for office space. This can be difficult if that room is also used for overnight guests, especially if your guests plan an extended stay. You will feel like an intruder when you need to get something from your office, and your guests may feel they're interfering in your business.

If the spare bedroom is rarely or never used for overnight guests and you don't plan on clients coming to this office space, by all means set up your office here.

People have turned large closets into their offices by building a computer station into the closet space. At the end of the day they close the closet/office door and can use the room for something else without the office being visible.

Partitions, Attics, and the Dining Room Table

If you're not fortunate enough to have a separate room, there are other ways to create a work environment for yourself. Use a variety of barriers to partition off a portion of a room—such as a bookcase, a room screen, or other furniture.

If at all possible, do not use the dining room table unless you never use the dining room. It is frustrating to have to move your work every time you have a meal.

A woman who took a home-based business class from Bev a few years ago was asking how to get her husband's cooperation and support. It appeared to her that not only wasn't he supportive, but in fact he made it difficult for her to operate her business in the home. After questioning her, Bev found out that she made jewelry on the dining room table and had her supplies stacked all over the room. They did not have eating space in the kitchen, and generally ate on trays in the family room. Bev suggested perhaps her husband wasn't happy about the extent her business was interfering with their personal life. A year later Bev heard that the woman and her husband had built her a work space in their attached garage and both were now happier with the arrangements.

This is just one case where lack of appropriate space and a lack of communication with other members of the household nearly shut down a home-based business. Your office space must be a place you can work without the stress of worrying about interfering in the family routine, and it should be situated so the family can feel free to continue their lives without interfering in your business.

We've known people who turned their sunroom into an office. If you and/or your family are willing to give up this space, it may be ideal. It should have lots of light. Make sure it's warm enough in the winter and not too warm in the summer.

As Bev writes this chapter, she's sitting in the sunroom of a rental house. The biggest problem for her is the amount of light that comes in the eight windows during the day. There is too much glare on the computer screen, so towels are tacked up on each window to cut down on the amount of light. There are double glass doors to the room, which help cut down on household noise, while allowing her to see what's going on in the rest of the house while she works.

Meanwhile, Don has divided his living room into two separate spaces, one for his personal area and one for his business. Living alone, he doesn't need to worry about other family members, so he has simply placed his office space where he has the best light and where his office is least intrusive on the rest of the living space.

Consider any space you might be able to partition off. For instance, a long hallway with a window at the end may give you enough space to create a work space if nothing else is available or you just like the space.

Attics can be gloomy, like basements, but with some remodeling they could become your office suite. Adding light and heat, if necessary, may give you the peace and quiet your business demands without requiring others in the household to give up community space.

Keep in mind that you may be able to change your space. A friend of Don's originally put her office in her basement because that was the only space in her house the family could spare. Once her daughter moved away to college, however, she moved her office into her daughter's vacated room upstairs.

The point, of course, is that where there's a will, there's a way. If a solution to office space doesn't easily present itself, be creative.

Refer back to Chapter 3, "Keeping It Legal," for details on what you must do in order to take a home office deduction on your taxes. This might impact some of the office space decisions you'll make.

Noise and Family Traffic

Some households are noisier than others. Children of preschool age generally have one volume level when playing—loud! Elementary age children like to watch cartoons after school or play video games. Both only seem to have one volume level—loud! Dogs barking, birds squawking, and vacuums running are all normal household noises. But, they are not normal office noises. When you live and work under the same roof, noise control can be an issue.

Numerous parents have told their children they would be working from home in order to spend more time with the family. Unfortunately, the time seems to be spent telling them to turn down the TV or stop running in the house because Mom or Dad is working and there's too much noise. Children and others in the house may come to resent the home-based business parent. Take these issues into consideration when deciding on your office location.

STORAGE

Depending on whether you have a service business or a product business, the amount of storage space you need varies. For a service business, your storage needs will primarily be client files and office supplies. Generally, a file cabinet and some shelves will be sufficient. If you have a separate room for your office, this shouldn't be a problem.

If, however, you're sharing a room with personal space, a file cabinet may not fit the decor. If there's a closet in the room, consider putting a file cabinet in there. You may need to consider two 2-drawer file cabinets instead of one 4-drawer so you can still use the hanging space. If there is no closet, find the least obtrusive space that is still handy to your work space. Perhaps two 2-drawer file cabinets with a piece of wood across the top would work for you. Check your local building supply store for an unfinished hollow core or solid core wooden interior door that may have a ding or a scratch in it—they usually don't have hinges yet and may or may not have the hole for the doorknob—that you can get for a reduced price. This is just about the right size to put across two 2-drawer file cabinets and the approximate height for a worktable or desk.

As your business expands, you may need to expand your storage area. Consider putting former client files in file boxes that can be stored out of the way but are still accessible.

If you have a product business, zoning ordinances may prohibit you from storing all your products on site. You may ask, "Who will know?" Maybe no one, unless you live in an area that allows periodic inspection of registered home-based businesses.

Product storage can be a problem for home-based businesses. It could be that products have taken over more rooms of the house than anticipated, creating problems that include arguments among the family members who feel displaced.

So what do you do? Some alternatives are:

- Consider another space in the house, such as a basement that can be remodeled to house your business.
- Build an addition to house your business or to give the family the space they need.
- Use a storage shed or portion of the garage.
- Rent storage space, hopefully nearby.

If your product business is taking over the house and interfering with your personal life, and none of the above-mentioned alternatives, or others, are possible, it may be time to consider moving to commercial space.

While we're talking about storage, you'll need a safe place to keep important papers such as insurance documents and tax returns for your business. A fireproof safe is one option. Since a small safe can run from $50 to $150 and more, it may seem like quite an expense at this time. Your other option is to rent a safe deposit box at your local bank. Rates run about $15 to $25 per year for a small box. The disadvantage of renting a safe deposit box is that you can only access your papers when the bank is open. A fireproof safe is always available, but at a higher cost. You are the best judge of what works best for you.

FURNISHINGS, CARPETS, LIGHTS, ETC.

Setting up your home office does not need to be an expensive venture. Too many new home-based business owners spend precious start-up funds buying a desk, chair, file cabinets, bookcases, telephone, etc. Unless you have unlimited funds, consider these alternatives to new furnishings:

- Used-furniture stores
- Yard sales

- Auctions, both local and online
- Classified ads
- Building your own

When Bev began her desktop publishing business, she set up an old desk in a corner of the room that her husband used as his library. The desk was big enough to hold her computer and keyboard but did not have much space for anything else. The printer sat on an old tea cart. As the business began to build, she added what was needed as she could afford it. A friend built her first drawing table for the price of the materials. A new client's business gave her the funds to purchase a laser printer. As the furnishings increased, space decreased, until her husband had to move out of his library into a spare bedroom that had recently been vacated by their son.

As the business continued to grow, she needed more storage and work space. She began attending auctions with her husband and found a fax stand for half the price of a new one. The best buy was her oak desk bought at auction for $65. It was less than a year old and cost $1,200 new. A storage unit came from a friend who was moving.

Because Bev spent so much time at her desk, she needed a good ergonomic chair. She found one that was returned to the local office supply store because it had a slight defect. It was half the original price and very fixable.

Over the years, Don has outfitted several different offices with furniture and fixtures procured from friends, bankruptcy auctions, going-out-of-business sales, and used-furniture stores. Our experiences demonstrate that you can outfit a functional, efficient office for minimal cost.

Equipping your office will be discussed in more detail in Chapter 7, "Outfitting a High-Tech Home Office."

Floor Coverings

Some people prefer hardwood floors in their home, while others prefer carpeting. Your office flooring is a personal preference also. Hardwood floors will make for a noisier work space, which may distract some people. If you're considering carpet for your office but don't need to upgrade the rest of the house carpeting, shop for carpet remnants. Often you can find a room-size rug that has been left over from another job that will fit your space. If you don't want the expense of having wall-to-wall carpeting installed, consider the cost of having the remnant bound on all sides and use it as an area rug.

If you do have carpeting in your home office, be aware of static electricity generated by friction. This can be lethal for your computer. Most office supply stores carry a hard plastic mat to put under your office chair. This also makes it easier to move your chair around when you have a carpeted floor.

The more time you spend thinking through your office setup, the better. You'll find it much easier to "go to work" if you like your office.

Electricity and Lighting

A computer uses a lot of electrical outlets for all its components. Depending on your business, you may have other electrical needs as well. If it's possible to upgrade your electrical service to add an additional circuit for the office space, you'll find it very helpful.

As far as lighting goes, generally the room or area you choose for your office will need additional sources of light. Consider task lighting such as desk lamps, or spot lighting, or halogen lights that will reflect off the ceiling. If possible, consider adding a dropped ceiling with fluorescent light fixtures or canned or recessed lighting to increase the amount of light for your office, particularly if your office is in the basement or a room with few or no windows.

YOUR PROFESSIONAL IMAGE

How do you answer your phone? If you said "Hello," that's the wrong answer. People at "real" businesses answer with the company name, which means to be taken seriously, you have to as well. If you only have one phone for both family and business, you need another phone or another number.

Ideally you should have a separate phone line for your business and a separate line for your computer and fax machine. It is possible to have numerous telephone numbers without having more lines. The service is called different things in different regions of the country but is generally known as "distinctive ring" service. You can have several different phone numbers that all sound a little different when they ring so you know which number is being called and can answer appropriately. The downside of this service is that all numbers will be busy (or voice mail services will pick up) whenever one of the numbers is being used.

Family members may think they're being helpful by answering your business phone, but discourage them if they cannot answer in a professional manner or take accurate messages. You are the best judge of the ability of others in your household to answer your business line.

The best solution for distinguishing business calls from personal calls is to have a separate phone line. Many are now using a cell phone for business instead of having a separate line put into the house. Note: Consider a hands-free headset for your office or cell phone. It's amazing what else you can get done when your hands are free while talking on the phone. It's also safer when driving, if you receive a call on your cell phone that you need to answer.

Make sure that however you decide to go with your business phone, your clients can leave a message when you're unavailable. And make sure you retrieve your messages on a regular basis and return those calls. That will go a long way toward creating credibility with your clients. Most telephone companies have a voice mail service for a reasonable monthly fee. Most cell phone services include voice mail either for free or for a small fee. When you record your outgoing message for voice mail, make sure there are no household noises in the background. Dogs barking, televisions blaring, or dishwashers running are not what clients want to hear in your message even if they know you're home-based. Remember, this is your professional image we're are talking about.

If you use e-mail, retrieve your messages at least twice a day and respond quickly. Set up a separate e-mail account for your business. Not having to wade through personal e-mails will make it easier to keep track of responses. As for "snail" mail, answer it promptly and follow up on any promises you make. Treat everyone the way you want to be treated.

Dressing to Suit the Part

The public sometimes perceives home-based business owners as sitting around in their underwear, drinking coffee and watching television. Your home may be your castle, but when it's also the office, you must dress the part. That doesn't mean you have to wear a business suit all the time, but you will want to dress a little less casually when there's a chance that you'll be seen by a client or vendor. And wearing business attire helps some people stay motivated.

Dressing the part also depends on what your business involves. First impressions can be hard to overcome, especially if they're negative. Attending a networking meeting in a sweatsuit may work for a personal trainer, but probably not a venture capital broker. As in most business settings, it's better to be slightly overdressed in an unknown situation than underdressed.

One caveat in the other direction, however: If you wear clothing in which you feel uncomfortable, people can tell. What they can't tell is whether you're uncomfortable about your product or service, or for some other reason. When going out in public, dress to balance comfort and impact.

Setting Hours

Although reasons for wanting to work from home are many and varied, most home-based business owners cite the ability to set their own hours as a major factor in their decision.

Your clients will need to know when they can reasonably expect to reach you in the office. And you will stay focused more easily if you set specific work hours for yourself. Posting your hours on the office door helps you and your family keep the boundaries. Stating your hours in your voice mail message will reduce the number of business calls "after hours." Adding a surcharge to your invoice for work the client expects you to perform outside your "normal" working hours is another way to train clients to your preferred work hours.

GETTING YOUR MAIL

You have four basic options for your company address:

1. Your home address
2. Post office box
3. Mail service company
4. Full-service executive suite company

Your Home Address

This is the easiest and least expensive option. You do not need to pay anybody to accept your mail for you, and you don't need to travel anywhere to pick it up. In addition, you get your mail in the timeliest fashion. If you see clients in your home, they can easily find you from the information on your business card and letterhead.

The first concern that most people have about using their home address is image related. They fear that prospects will be able to tell that their business is home-based and may not take them seriously. Most people are unable to tell whether a particular address is residential or commercial. However, the prevalent attitude when they discover that you are home-based is one of envy and curiosity. If you act professionally, they won't care that your business is home-based. If they do act with disdain when finding out, either write them off as someone you would rather not do business with anyway or dazzle them with your professional brilliance by presenting your portfolio or a copy of your client list with testimonials. If they still act as if you aren't worth considering, definitely write them off!

Post Office Box

Post office boxes traditionally have been used by home-based businesses to disguise their being home-based. As it becomes more acceptable and legal to operate out of your home, it's not necessary to use a post office box. If you get a large volume of mail, regular packages, etc., a P.O. box may be a more workable alternative. Keep in mind that only items sent via the postal service can be left at a P.O. box. This means that UPS, FedEx, and other carriers will need to deliver packages to a different address, reducing the convenience of a P.O. box.

Mail Service Company

The ability to accept deliveries from any carrier is one of the advantages of using a mail service company such as the UPS Store or Parcel Plus. Another is that they can provide you with additional help with your shipping needs. But perhaps the most significant benefit for most home-based business owners is that you will have a street address, typically in a commercial district. In the past, your box number was listed as a suite number. However, a few years ago it was made mandatory that suite numbers be replaced with PMB for Personal Mail Box. The reason was to cut down on mail fraud.

Box rentals at mail service companies are significantly more expensive than at post offices. There are also fewer mail service locations than there are post offices, so it's likely that you'll have to drive farther to pick up your mail.

Full-Service Executive Suite

Your fourth option is a full-service executive suite. These companies typically are located at high-profile commercial addresses and occupy a full floor of a nice building. In addition to acting as a mail drop, the companies offer phone answering, faxing, and space to hold meetings.

The prices you pay at these companies will primarily depend on what services you want to use. Unlike mail service companies, whose prices are fairly close to each other, executive suite rates vary widely. But the costs at a suite company will consistently be higher than at a mail service company.

INSURANCE

Now let's talk about something most people don't even think about, or if they do, they assume it's taken care of—insurance. After spending all this time and effort locating and setting up your office, you want to make sure your furnishings, lighting, equipment, and the rest are covered by insurance. Don't assume your homeowners insurance will cover your business in the home. In most cases, if you have any coverage for the business, it's minimal. In addition to insuring your equipment (and inventory if you have it), you'll need business-related liability insurance in case a client or others coming to your home business gets injured on your property.

In-Home Business

Bev had a near catastrophe in the early years of her desktop publishing business. A cracked storm window fell out of the frame from a second story window onto the front porch of her house. This was the door clients used when coming to her business. If someone had been standing there when the glass fell, they would have been seriously injured, or possibly killed. She'd never thought about insurance up to that point, but a quick call to her insurance agent changed all that. She quickly added an umbrella to her current homeowners policy, covering her equipment and adding additional liability for personal injury. A mere seven months later, her house was struck by lightning during a particularly bad thunderstorm. In addition to damaged electronics, outlets, and even a hole in the living room wall, every piece of equipment in her office was literally fried by the surge of electricity. Without the recent insurance policy, Bev would probably have been out of business at that point. Thanks to the insurance, after paying the deductible and spending six weeks researching new equipment, her office was better equipped than ever.

No one ever thinks his or her house will catch on fire or have lightning strike it. Bev certainly didn't. But it's not worth the risk for the small price you'll pay for an in-home business policy. Because it is your home, things can happen that you wouldn't necessarily expect in commercial space. Is your office located below a bathroom floor? Showers and toilets overflow. If your office is nearby, you may have a catastrophe. Don't take things for granted. Get the insurance.

Automobile

In addition to the in-home business insurance, you will need to check your automobile insurance for appropriate coverage. Depending on the type of business you operate and the type of vehicle you drive, you may have to purchase an additional or separate policy. Your insurance agent will be able to advise you.

Health Insurance

Health insurance is a particularly difficult subject. Everyone needs it, few can afford it on their own, and too many people in the United States today are without it. For many home-based business owners this has been the breaking point for closing down a business. It is just too expensive to handle on your own. Hopefully, the day will come when there are more affordable health insurance options available to individuals. Until then, if you don't have health insurance coverage under a spouse's plan, there are a few things you can do.

First, if you're leaving a company where you are covered by health insurance, ask about COBRA. It is more expensive than what you may have been paying for your insurance, but it's still cheaper than an individual health insurance policy. You can only be on COBRA for 18 months, but this will give you time to shop around for another policy.

If your business is a C Corporation (refer to Chapter 3 for the different business structures), you are an employee of the company and may be able to qualify for a group insurance rate for yourself and your family.

Check with the organizations you belong to or plan to join. Many have group insurance policies for their members that are reasonable, although probably still higher than what you were paying as an employee contribution.

Other Insurance Needs

Once your business has begun to grow, keep in touch with your insurance agent and update him or her regularly on changes. For instance, if you have a home repair business and are constantly buying expensive tools, you may want to increase your equipment insurance. If you're dependent on your business income, you may want to look into income replacement or disability insurance in case something happens that prohibits you from earning that income for a period of time. The premiums are based on your previous business income and the amount of time between your injury or illness and your policy kicking in. The longer you can wait before taking advantage of the insurance, the lower your premium will be.

Ask your insurance agent about discounts. Often you will get a better rate by having all your insurance needs covered by the same company. In some cases, one company may not offer all the different types of insurance you need. An independent insurance agent can shop around for you to get the best policy at the best price.

MOVING OUT OF THE HOME OFFICE

This may seem an odd subject to you at this point, since you're just beginning your home-based business. However, inevitably the question comes up about outgrowing the home office space. Informal research shows that the majority of home-based business owners don't anticipate moving out of the home anytime in the future. If they do move out, it is generally sooner than later. For instance, the new home-based business owner finds that he or she is just not suited to working from home.

There are several other reasons why a home-based business owner might move the business out of the home. The number one reason is zoning restrictions. According to the American Planning Association, the most common restrictions by zoning ordinance that cause a business to be moved from the home (or not started there in the first place) are:

- Restrictions on vehicular traffic
- Restrictions on on-street parking
- Restrictions on use or size of outside signs
- Limitations on employees
- Limitations on floor space allowed for the business
- Restrictions on materials storage

The second most common reason a home-based business owner might move the business out of the house is growth. Some home-based business owners deliberately restrict the growth of their business for this reason. Others move to a bigger house in order to accommodate the business expansion. However, others simply find they prefer to move into commercial space.

Working at home may not work for your family. You may feel pulled in too many directions to concentrate on your business, and your finances might be suffering as well as your personal relationships. If you feel there's no other alternative to this situation, moving the business may be your only choice.

Chapter 7

OUTFITTING A HIGH-TECH HOME OFFICE

Choosing the Right Technology for Your Business

Advancements in technology have arguably had more impact in the growth of home-based businesses than any other factor. The combination of ever-more powerful products and ever-lower costs has made once-sophisticated technology available to the average home-business owner. Today you could conceivably outfit a home office with all the computer equipment it needs for under $1,000. On the other hand, you could also spend thousands more, depending on the hardware, software, and peripherals you choose.

So how do you know what to buy? What do you need immediately and what can you put off until you have more cash available? And what must you not overlook?

This chapter will review your options for each of several technology products and services and point out specific things to look for. We have avoided mentioning specific models and version numbers because of the rapid pace of change in all areas of the technology sector.

Before you buy, we recommend getting as much information as you can to help you make the best possible decision. Your hardware and software products are among your biggest investments, and you'll have to live and work with them for a long time. Talk with friends, relatives, and especially other business owners about their experiences. Read magazines, including:

- *Consumer Reports*
- *Home Office Computing*

- *Mac Addict*
- *MacHome*
- *Macworld*
- *Maximum PC*
- *PC Magazine*
- *PC World*
- *Smart Computing*

Several major electronics retailers have useful information and product reviews on their Web sites. Check out:

- Best Buy: www.bestbuy.com
- Circuit City: www.circuitcity.com
- CompUSA: www.compusa.com

And for the latest and most comprehensive information, reviews, and product comparisons, log some time at these Web sites:

- CNET: www.cnet.com
- DealTime: www.dealtime.com
- Price Grabber: www.pricegrabber.com
- ZDNet: www.zdnet.com

HARDWARE

For the technologically challenged, the term *hardware* simply refers to computers and computer-related equipment, as opposed to *software*, which refers to the programs that run on the computers. In other words, hardware is physical while software is virtual.

Computer

When choosing your computer for your business, you have two basic issues to decide on: desktop versus laptop and Windows versus Mac.

The first decision should be fairly straightforward. If you're going to set your computer down on a desk and just leave it there, a desktop model is going to give you more power and features for a lower price. If you plan on traveling, however, or if you'd like the freedom to move your computer from room to room or even outside (like we do), then a laptop is a must.

The second issue can be a little trickier. In part it depends on what you're used to. If you're already comfortable with one system, stick with it. There's no point in learning a whole new operating system if you don't have to.

If you don't already have a preference, you'll want to weigh other factors and determine what's most important to you. Apple's products are easier to learn, simpler to use, and don't crash as often. And Macs have always been superior for graphics work. Windows machines, on the other hand, give you more choices. There is a lot more software available for Windows than for Mac, although the most popular business programs are available for both. Windows will also give you more choice in manufacturers whether you go the laptop or desktop route. And because of the competition, Windows computers are typically less expensive than comparable Macs.

Choosing a Desktop Computer

When buying a desktop system, the rule of thumb is to avoid the extremes. A computer at the low end of the price spectrum is likely to incorporate a lot of compromises that will frustrate you sooner or later. Probably sooner. On the other hand, a model at the bleeding edge is likely to be more computer than you need, and subsequently not worth the extra money. That still leaves a lot of systems by a lot of manufacturers in the middle range to choose from, which is where you'll get your best value. While there are dozens of features to sift and sort through, these are the most important ones:

- *Processor speed—measured in gigahertz (GHz).* All things being equal, the faster the processor (the CPU chip), the faster the computer works. But faster processors are being introduced almost every month. Which means that the top-of-the-line chips are sold at a premium while processors that held the title last month are much more reasonably priced. This gives you an opportunity to save some money. All but the slowest processors on the market are sufficient for your business needs. Choose a chip in the middle range and you'll get a good deal on a processor that's plenty fast enough.
- *Memory—measured in megabytes (MB) or gigabytes (GB).* Computer memory is often referred to as RAM, an acronym for random-access memory. It's where computers store software programs and data that are currently in use. As a result, it's the other major factor besides processor speed that affects your computer's performance. The more memory your computer has, the more applications and files you can work on at once. There are various permutation of RAM, including DRAM, SDRAM, and RDRAM. Don't worry about the differences among the types—they're marginal. Just be sure to buy as much RAM as you can afford.

- *Hard drive.*   The hard drive is your long-term storage. It's where you save all your files. The two important characteristics of a hard drive are its capacity, measured in gigabytes (GB), and its rotational speed, measured in revolutions per minute (rpm). The bigger and faster, the better. Of course, the bigger and faster, the more expensive too. And hard drive prices go up sharply as their capacity increases marginally. A midrange hard drive should give you plenty of storage at an affordable price. However, if you're going to be working with a lot of photo, sound, or video files, you'll want to get one at the upper end of the storage scale.
- *Optical drive.*   This is the CD or DVD drive. Most CD drives that are sold these days are recordable (CD-R) drives that both play and record (or "write" or "burn") CDs. A CD-R drive has three different speeds: writing, rewriting, and reading. You'll see numbers like 24x/10x/40x. These numbers tell the speeds of the drive relative to the speeds of the first-generation drives. So a drive labeled 24x/10x/40x writes at 24 times the speed of first-generation drives, rewrites at 10 times the speed, and reads at 40 times the speed. (We know, it makes no sense. It's a geek thing.) The faster the write speed of your drive, the less time it will take you to burn CDs. You'll want to either get a DVD drive as well or a combo CD-R/DVD drive, which will both record CDs and play DVDs. A recordable DVD drive is even better, if you can afford it, because you can store so much more data on a DVD than a CD.
- *Reliability and support.*   What you want is *not* a home computer. And it's not a computer for a business with lots of computers, any of which you could borrow if yours were to fail. This is a computer for your home business. If it goes down, you go down. So you need a reliable machine to minimize the chance of failure and good technical support in case something does go wrong. You can get an idea about a manufacturer's reliability by reading reviews and asking others who have the same machine.

Choosing a Laptop Computer

Any laptop is a set of trade-offs. The more power and features, the heavier and more expensive. The smaller it is, the harder the keyboard is to use and the less you can see on the screen. To choose the right laptop for you, you'll need to prioritize your needs and wants. In addition to the items listed for desktops, consider these factors:

- Screen size—measured diagonally in inches
- Display quality and brightness

- Weight—measured in pounds, but *without* its AC power adapter
- Battery life
- Number and types of ports
- Ruggedness
- Type of pointing device
- Number and swapability of drive bays

Computer Accessories

There are several types of items that can make your computer safer, more versatile, and more convenient. Some are purely optional, while the last item in this list—a backup system—is absolutely critical. The more you use your computer, the more each of these accessories will make a difference to you.

Monitor

The monitor that comes with your computer may be just fine. But if it's not, or if you're buying a system where you can pick and choose each component, you have two basic types of monitor to choose from: cathode-ray tube (CRT) or liquid-crystal display (LCD).

CRTs are the traditional big, bulky monitors. And the bigger they are, the more of your desk they take up. But they're cheaper than LCDs of the same size, brighter, and they display colors more accurately. LCD monitors are flat-panel displays that require very little space even in large screen sizes. They consume less energy, cause less eyestrain, and don't get as hot as CRTs, but they can be budget busters, especially at the higher end.

Keyboard

If you're going to be doing a lot of typing on your laptop, it may make sense to buy a full-size keyboard, especially if that's what you're accustomed to using. And even if you're using a desktop computer, it may be worthwhile to buy a wireless keyboard that you can use in any position you want, or an ergonomic keyboard to prevent wrist fatigue and strain. Bev has used a wireless keyboard by Logitech for several years and loves its flexibility.

Mouse

The mouse that comes with your computer is likely to be very basic. And on a laptop, a mouse won't even be included because you'll have some other, less accurate pointing device built into the unit. So if you don't love the mouse or pointing device that came with your computer, buy a better one.

There are dozens on the market in a wide range of shapes, sizes, and prices. You'll find wireless mice, mice designed for left-handed users, and many other features. If you're going to be carrying your laptop on the road, buy a small travel mouse. Don particularly likes the Kensington PocketMouse Pro, with its retractable cord. Bev uses a wireless mouse, also by Logitech, with her laptop and desktop machines.

Remote Control

If you're going to be using your laptop to give slide presentations, invest in a wireless handheld remote control. It allows you to run your computer without having to stand right next to it. Which means you can advance slides from wherever you are in the room. Very cool.

Uninterruptible Power System

If you've ever lost an important piece of computer work because of a power failure, you'll understand the need for an uninterruptible power system, or UPS. A UPS is basically a large battery that automatically powers the hardware that's plugged into it whenever your house's power is lost. Generally speaking, the more expensive the UPS, the more items that can be plugged in and the longer it will supply power.

A UPS is absolutely necessary for a desktop computer. A small UPS is sufficient to give you enough time to save your work and shut your computer down safely. If you need your computer to run continuously, you'll want to invest in a larger UPS.

For a laptop, a UPS is typically unnecessary because the laptop's battery will automatically supply power if the AC power is cut off. However, do make sure that your laptop—and all other electronic equipment—is plugged into a good surge protector to keep it safe from electrical spikes.

Wireless Network

If you're going to be moving your computer from room to room or if you'll be using more than one computer, you may want to consider installing a wireless local area network (LAN) in your home. You can pay a computer network consultant to put your LAN together for you or you can do it yourself. You can find everything you need at your local computer store and set up your LAN within an hour or two. Bev set up two computers in her office so they could share files and share a single Internet connection. It took her about an hour to insert the hardware into the two computers and install the software.

Backup Systems

Many home-business owners fail to back up the contents of their computers because they believe it's a waste of time and energy. After all, nothing's going to happen to *them*.

Don't be one of the misguided who realizes the value of backing up your computer only after something has happened to your data. What could happen? Consider the possibilities:

- Your computer could be dropped on the floor.
- Your house could catch fire.
- Your house could be destroyed by a natural disaster.
- Your computer could be damaged in a car accident.
- Someone could steal your computer.
- You could suffer a random computer crash.
- Your computer could get fried by a lightning strike.
- Your kids could play with your computer and accidentally delete files.
- Someone could spill liquid on your computer.
- Your computer could contract a virus.

For the average person, a loss of files and data can be a major inconvenience. For your business, it can be catastrophic. Fortunately, there are a wide variety of backup systems that make it easier than ever to protect your valuable data. Your options include:

- Magnetic discs such as Zip or Jaz
- Optical discs such as CDs and DVDs
- Magnetic tape
- A second computer
- Online services that store your data on the Web

Which option (or options) you choose depends on what you're already familiar with, what your computer is equipped with, your storage needs, and your budget. Whatever you decide on, be sure to keep a copy of your data somewhere other than your home.

Peripherals and Other Electronics

Your computer is probably the most important piece of electronic equipment in your home office, but it isn't the only one you'll need. Printers, copiers, and other items are what make a spare bedroom a true office.

As with computers, avoid the low end as a general rule. Products at the cheap end of the price scale frequently turn out to be much less of a bargain than they seemed originally. If your budget is really tight, consider buying used or refurbished equipment instead.

Printer

While there can seem to be a confusing number of choices in printers, there are basically two kinds to choose from: ink-jets and laser printers. Each one is a proven technology and each has its particular strengths.

Ink-jet printers shoot tiny droplets of ink from one or more cartridges onto the page to produce text and images. The biggest advantages of ink-jet printers are their versatility and their low price. Ink-jets enable you to print both black-and-white and color with an inexpensive machine. The drawbacks are that print speed is slower than a laser, the print quality is not as good, and the ink cartridges are expensive to replace, making the cost per page high.

Laser printers work much like a photocopier, using a drum and toner, then fusing the toner to the paper. The advantages of a laser printer are fast print speeds, low cost per page, and sharp, crisp text and graphics. The primary drawbacks are that they are more expensive than ink-jets and most of them only print in black-and-white.

If you can afford it and have the space, consider buying both. You'll get the most printing options and the best quality for different needs. Or for a little more money you may want to go with a color laser. It's more expensive than two moderately priced printers, but it will save you space and give you amazing output.

Whatever route you choose, here are the features to compare:

- Print speed—measured in pages per minute (ppm)
- Resolution—measured in dots per inch (dpi) vertically and horizontally
- Paper capacity
- Memory—measured in kilobytes (KB) or megabytes (MB)
- Ink cartridge or toner cartridge life

Scanner

A scanner is handy for converting hard copies into digital image files that you can store and work with on your computer. Your basic choice is between a sheet-fed (upright) and a flatbed scanner. A sheet-fed takes up less space on your desk, but a flatbed allows you to scan odd-sized or odd-shaped items. As you're looking, consider these factors:

- Optical resolution—measured in dots per inch (dpi) vertically and horizontally
- Color depth—measured in bits
- Maximum scan area

Fax Machine

With the growth of e-mail, faxing has become less important, but a fax machine is still a necessity for transmitting hard copies of documents. Fortunately, the days of thermal paper rolls are behind us. Some machines on the market still use thermal transfer technology, but they do it with plain paper. Pretty much everything available these days will do a good job whether it's a thermal, ink-jet, or laser machine. Here are the features to compare:

- Transmission speed—in pages per minute (ppm)
- Auto-document feeder (and its capacity)
- Paper tray capacity
- Memory—measured in kilobytes (KB) or megabytes (MB)
- Print cartridge life

Copier

A photocopier is pretty much a necessity for any home office. Fortunately for us, costs have come down while features have gone up. And there are copiers to fit any budget. The most important factors to consider are:

- Speed—in copies per minute (cpm)
- Paper tray capacity
- Auto-document feeder (and its capacity)
- Warm-up time
- Stationary or moving platen
- Maximum original document size
- Enlargement and reduction
- Toner replacement costs

Multifunction Printer

There was a time when a multifunction printer (MFP) represented a serious compromise. While it combined a printer, scanner, copier, and sometimes even a fax machine into one unit, it didn't do any of those things particularly well. But as technology has progressed, multifunction machines have made tremendous strides.

While today's MFPs still can't match top-of-the-line single-purpose machines in features or performance, they are much less of a compromise than they used to be. Their options and results now range from reasonable to excellent. You do pay a price for that improvement. A good MFP costs hundreds more than any single-purpose unit, but less than buying three or four mid-range peripherals. And the space you save in your home office is a huge side benefit.

The only other caveat is that if your multifunction machine breaks, you lose all its functions. If that thought scares you, or if you have very specific high-end needs for your equipment, you're better off buying individual peripherals. Otherwise, for both budget and space reasons, a good MFP is an excellent choice.

Like printers, MFPs are available in ink-jet and laser models. Ink-jet machines are considerably cheaper, but laser models produce much sharper copies.

Personal Digital Assistant

In the old days, choosing a personal digital assistant (PDA) was easy. You just bought a Palm Pilot. Today there's incredible variety in the PDA market.

There are PDAs with built-in cameras, voice recorders, or MP3 players. Some models integrate a wireless phone that also gives you e-mail and Web browsing capability. Some include a miniature keyboard, allowing you to "type" as well as handwrite notes with a stylus. And Microsoft's Pocket PC operating system (OS) has challenged Palm by enabling PDAs to run the most popular business programs, turning them into miniature PCs and giving new meaning to the term *handheld*.

The first step in picking a PDA is deciding what you want to do with it. Do you just want something to store names and addresses along with your to-do list, or do you want all the bells and whistles? Or something in between? Think about how you'll actually use it.

Next, decide if you want the Palm OS or the Microsoft OS. The operating system you choose will determine what programs you can run on your PDA and will instantly narrow down your manufacturer choices.

Finally, compare these features:

- Battery type and life
- Size and weight
- Memory
- Expansion slots and type of expansion cards

- Resolution
- Number of colors supported

Digital Camera

A camera can be a useful business tool. You can take pictures of your products, your customers, the results of your work, and more. You can use those photos in newsletters, press releases, flyers, brochures, and catalogs. You can put them on memo pads, coffee mugs, calendars, your Web site, postcards, and T-shirts.

A digital camera makes all this easy because all you have to do is upload the images directly into your computer. No film, no processing, no scanning.

With all the benefits, the decision to buy a digital camera is easy. The decision about which one to buy, however, can be difficult. With a bewildering array of cameras on the market manufactured by both camera companies (Nikon, Canon, Pentax, Olympus, Kodak, Fuji, Minolta) and computer companies (Hewlett-Packard, Sony, Toshiba), choosing the right one for you and your business can seem a daunting task. Especially when several new cameras are introduced every month.

Talk to friends and relatives about their cameras. Read reviews and comparisons in magazines and Web sites. And above all, go to a camera or electronics store to play with them for yourself. See how the camera feels in your hand, and ask questions until you're satisfied with the answers. Here are some things to consider when shopping for a digital camera:

- Picture quality—measured in megapixels
- Optical zoom (you can pretty much ignore less important digital zoom claims)
- Number and types of preset modes
- Storage type and capacity
- Battery type and life
- Size and weight

Cell Phone

If you've had to leave your company cell phone behind and need to get your own, you have a lot to choose from. But the choice of phone is less important than the choice of service provider. Investigate providers in your area and ask friends about their experiences. You want to compare:

- Coverage areas
- Rate plans
- Services provided
- Customer service

Don is a huge fan of AT&T Wireless because of their coverage and customer service, while Bev loves U.S. Cellular for the same reasons.

After you've decided on a service provider, pick a rate plan based on how you expect to use your phone. And finally, choose the phone itself, based on:

- Battery type and life
- Size and weight
- Keypad
- Display screen

SOFTWARE

Your computer is pretty useless until you load some software on it. And if you thought choosing a computer was difficult, you ain't seen nothin' yet. There are thousands of software titles on the market, produced by hundreds of companies. Which ones do you really need, and which ones can you leave on the shelf?

To help you figure out what should be on your shopping list, we've organized the most important types of software for a home-based business into 13 categories. Within each category, we've listed the most popular and widely available programs, along with the name of the manufacturer in parentheses.

As you shop, keep in mind that many programs come in several variations, including Standard, Pro, Platinum, Deluxe, and more. Also, companies often merge or buy another company's products, so manufacturer and program names can change at any time.

Accounting

As we will discuss in the next chapter, "Starting at the Top," accounting is one the seven crucial functions that must be performed in your business. Accounting software will make it much easier, both for you and your accountant. You can generate invoices, track time spent on projects, record payments, and keep track of expenses, as well as create all kinds of useful reports, charts, and graphs that will give you important insights into the financial state of your business.

Choosing the right accounting software for your home-based business depends on three factors:

1. The complexity of your business's finances
2. How familiar and comfortable you are with accounting
3. Which software your accountant uses

So talk with your accountant first. It will save you a lot of time and money if you use the same software package because, if nothing else, at the end of the year you make a copy of your financial files and e-mail or snail mail it to your accountant. He can simply load it onto his machine and prepare your returns for you quicker than if he has to enter all the data. If he only uses one program, it's probably best that you go with that one. If he uses two or more, he can help you figure out which one is right for you.

A subcategory of accounting software is tax preparation programs. These software packages enable you or your accountant to prepare your tax returns faster and easier, saving you time, effort, and money. Look for a program made by the same company as your accounting program, or one that supports your accounting program. That way you can be sure they work together and you won't have to learn a whole new program.

The major accounting and tax software programs are:

- MYOB Plus (MYOB)
- MYOB AccountEdge for Mac (MYOB)
- Peachtree Accounting (Peachtree)
- QuickBooks (Intuit)
- Simply Accounting (ACCPAC)
- TaxCut (Block Financial)
- Turbo Tax (Intuit)

Antivirus

Do we even need to make a case for getting an antivirus program? We didn't think so. One thing we will say, though, is make sure you update your virus definitions frequently, at least once every two weeks. New viruses are released almost every day, and your antivirus program needs to be kept up to date to recognize them.

The two category leaders are:

- MacAfee VirusScan (McAfee)
- Norton AntiVirus (Symantec)

Business Planning

If you'd like some interactive guidance in building your business plan, there are several programs that will walk you through the process:

- Biz Plan Builder (Jian)
- Business Plan Pro (Palo Alto)
- PlanWrite Business Plan Writer Deluxe (Nova Development)
- Professional Business Planmaker Deluxe (Individual Software)

CD and DVD Creation

When you buy a computer containing a CD-R or DVD-R drive, it will have some kind of recording software preinstalled on it. But if you plan to create CDs or DVDs for distribution or sale, you'll want to purchase a separate, full-featured CD/DVD creation program. Not only will it give you a lot more options for burning your discs, it will help you design professional-looking labels, covers, and inserts.

Consider these popular programs:

- Easy CD Creator (Roxio)
- Final Cut Express (Apple)
- Nero Burning ROM (Ahead Software)
- Instant CD-DVD (Pinnacle Systems)
- RecordNow Max (Stomp)

Communication

While your office suite software (see below) will come with an e-mail program, you may want to consider using Eudora, a full-featured, stand-alone e-mail package that is less susceptible to many viruses. And if you want to fax documents, WinFax Pro has long been the standard in full-featured faxing software.

- Eudora (QUALCOMM)
- WinFax Pro (Symantec)

Contact Management

In order to keep track of prospects, vendors, and customers, you need a contact manager. A contact manager is a specialized database that enables you to . . . well, um, manage your contacts. It does more than just act as an electronic address book, though. Much more. A good contact manager lets you:

- Schedule appointments
- Store a person's complete contact information
- Remind yourself of meetings, phone calls, and activities
- Keep track of birthdays, anniversaries, and other important dates
- Create to-do lists
- Track sales activity
- Review buying patterns and history
- Find people's contact information quickly
- Search your database by almost any criteria
- Create all kinds of sales reports

The key with a contact manager, of course, is using it consistently. Otherwise, it's not going to help you much. If you don't already have experience with your contact management program, take a class from a computer store or your local adult education system to familiarize yourself with the software, its navigation, and its capabilities. Then use it religiously.

The top three full-featured contact managers are:

- ACT! (Interact Commerce Corporation)
- Goldmine (FrontRange Solutions)
- Maximizer (Maximizer Software)

Desktop Publishing

For writing letters, contracts, and reports, a word processor is fine. But for creating newsletters, flyers, or other documents requiring layouts and graphics, a desktop publishing program is far superior. These are the four most popular software packages:

- Acrobat (Adobe)
- PageMaker (Adobe)
- Publisher (Microsoft)
- Quark xPress (Quark)

Graphic Design

Unless you're at least a competent designer, it's best to leave graphic work to a professional, as we'll discuss in Chapter 10, "Getting the World to Beat a Path to Your Door." As a home-based business, one of your most critical needs is to project a professional image. Amateurish graphic design undermines that image and causes people to take you less seriously. But if you're a pretty good designer and want to do some or all of your design work your-self, these programs will help:

- CorelDRAW (Corel)
- Designer (Corel)
- FreeHand MX (Macromedia)
- Illustrator (Adobe)
- Paint Shop Pro (Jasc)
- Painter (Corel)

Office Suites

Office suites combine some of the most commonly used business software programs into one bundle. They typically include some combination of a word processor, spreadsheet, database, Internet browser, e-mail client, and presentation software. The top four are:

- AppleWorks for Macintosh (Apple)
- Lotus SmartSuite (IBM)
- Office (Microsoft)
- WordPerfect Office (Corel)

Photo Editing

The popularity of digital photography and the versatility of digital images have led to an explosion of photo editing software. These programs enable you to manipulate digital photos in almost any way imaginable. There are programs aimed at novices, experts, and everyone in between. Look for one that fits your skill level among:

- ACDSee (ACD Systems)
- After Shot (Jasc)
- iPhoto (Apple)
- Kai's Photo Soap 2 (ScanSoft)
- Paint Shop Pro (Jasc)
- Photo Paint (Corel)
- PhotoImpact (Ulead)
- Photoshop (Adobe)
- PhotoSuite (Roxio)
- Picture It! (Microsoft)

Speech Recognition

If you hate to type, or if typing is physically challenging for you, a speech recognition program can be very valuable. Be forewarned that these programs take some time to adjust to, and require some time to adjust to you. And while they have made tremendous strides since they were first introduced, they're still a long way from perfect. Your two basic options are:

- Dragon Naturally Speaking (ScanSoft)
- ViaVoice (IBM)

Utilities

These are the programs that keep your computer running smoothly. Think of them as a maid service and a handyman for your computer. While there are hundreds of different utility programs available, the most popular are these bundles from McAfee and Symantec:

- McAfee Office (McAfee)
- Norton SystemWorks (Symantec)
- Norton Utilities (Symantec)

Web Design

Designing your Web site is another job that, ideally, should be left to professionals (see "Choosing a Web Design Company," below). The time and expertise required to create an effective Web site is significant. But if you feel you know enough about computers, design, and marketing and want to do it yourself, or if you'd like to be able to make changes to your site whenever you want, consider these options:

- Dreamweaver MX (Macromedia)
- FrontPage (Microsoft)
- Net Objects Fusion (Website Pros)
- Studio MX Plus (Macromedia)

Final Note on Software

Software makers are constantly updating, revising, and improving their products. There are two main reasons for this. One, they need to stay ahead of the competition in a cutthroat market. And two, they get to sell the same products to the same customers every year or two. (What a deal!)

Don't get caught up in upgrade fever. Just because there's a new version available doesn't mean you need to buy it. Unless you have specific needs or issues that a new version resolves, you can typically wait two, three, or more years before upgrading really makes sense, especially when you consider that you'll have to relearn the software each time. You'll save time and money while staying just as productive.

CHOOSING AN INTERNET SERVICE PROVIDER

You probably already have an Internet service provider (ISP) for your home. But that service may not be right for your home business. When you work at home, you need a service that can keep you connected to the Internet all or most of the day without tying up a phone line. You also need a connection that's faster than the typical dial-up home service so you don't waste valuable work time waiting for Web pages to download. And you need an ISP that's conducive to your professional image.

Which means you want to avoid the world's most popular online provider, AOL (America Online). Not that we have anything against AOL. It's easy to use, has lots of useful features, and is the most convenient ISP to access on the road if you travel a lot. It's just not the right choice for your home-based business. Because AOL is known as a consumer service, your business will be perceived as less professional if your e-mail address is your-business@AOL.com. Instead, you want to purchase a domain name for your business and use yourname@yourcompany.com as your e-mail address.

So, odds are you need a new ISP for your business. While there are a number of options besides dial-up services—ISDN, cable, DSL, and T-1 and T-3 lines—many of them may not be viable for you. T-1 and T-3 lines are simply much too expensive for the average home-based business, and some of the other high-speed services may not be available in your area.

So the first step is to find out what your local options are. Check with your phone company and cable company as well as other local and national ISPs. Depending on where you live and in what kind of building (many condominium complexes have exclusive agreements with a single online provider), you many only have one high-speed option. If you have more than that, weigh price against customer service and speed. Just as you can never be too rich or too thin, your online connection can never be too fast.

If you have no high-speed options, or you simply can't afford it, compare local and national ISPs. Since speed won't be an issue, compare price, customer service, and, if you travel, number of nationwide access numbers. And be sure to install a separate line for your Internet connection so you don't have to worry about missing calls while you're working online.

CHOOSING A WEB DESIGNER

There is probably no industry in which there's less correlation between what you pay and what you get than Web design. For $10,000 you can get a great site or a lousy site. We've seen terrific sites that cost $50,000, $5,000, and $500. All kinds of people—from computer programmers to graphic designers, from kids in school to retired seniors—have hung out shingles declaring themselves to be "Web designers."

Because of this characteristic of the industry, and because your Web site is one of your most important marketing tools, you need to take the Latin phrase *caveat emptor* ("buyer beware") to heart. Be very careful and thorough when evaluating Web design companies. Hiring one that's wrong for your business could be a very expensive mistake.

To increase your odds of finding a good, yet reasonably priced Web design company, start by asking other business owners for referrals. When you do, be sure to ask them what they like most and least about their own site and about what kind of results their site has brought them. If a business owner tells you their Web design company is great, but they have no idea if their site is working, that's not as strong a referral as someone who can tell you how much of their revenue stream and customer base their site is responsible for.

When you're interviewing Web design companies, ask to see examples of their work. The best fit is likely to be a company that's worked with businesses that are like yours in some way. And ask the designers what kind of results their sites have brought clients—because you should be more concerned with results than with how many animated images they've used on a site.

Here are some other questions to ask your potential Web designers:

- What is your philosophy about effective Web design?
- What is your design background?
- Do you have any marketing experience or expertise?
- How many people work in the company and what do they do?
- Do you do all the work in-house or do you outsource some of it?
- What programming software tools do you use?
- What do you use most frequently?
- Do you provide hosting or is that separate?

- How do you enable e-commerce?
- What is your approach to search engines?
- How do you keep up with changes in the Internet and Web design?
- How long have you been in business?
- What kinds of clients do you specialize in?
- Can I talk with some of your customers?

Since maintaining and updating your site is tremendously important (as we'll discuss in Chapter 10), you'll also want to ask about your options in this area. For example, if you want to make changes yourself, will you be able to, and how? If they must make changes, what fees are involved? And how often will they make changes for you?

The more questions you ask, the more likely you are to find a company that can build a great Web site for you at the right price. You've got plenty of choices in companies—take the time and the effort to make a good one.

Chapter 8

STARTING
AT THE TOP

Making the Leap from
Employee to CEO

When you are an employee of a company, you have one job. It may be broad, it may require you to do a lot of different activities, and it may challenge you to learn new skills. But you're basically working in one area of specialty, and you have other people to contribute their particular expertise or at least to share the workload.

When you run your own home-based business, however, everything changes. You are now responsible for every function a company needs to be successful. You are the sole decision maker. You're also the person ultimately responsible for how, and even *if*, things get done.

This transition from one role to many is arguably the single biggest challenge for the new home-based business owner. It requires you to change your ways of thinking, your work habits, and your skill sets. Many entrepreneurs discover too late the differences between performing a job and running a company. And nothing you've ever done as an employee completely prepares you for the switch.

The reason is that as an employee of a company you are typically filling one and only one role. As an *owner* of a company, you can't fill just that role, because your business needs more than that to survive. Every business, no matter how large or how small, has seven distinct needs that must be met. Which means there are seven different roles that must be filled to attend to those needs.

THE SEVEN ROLES

These are the seven roles that must be filled in any company:

1. Producer
2. Marketer
3. Salesperson
4. Accountant
5. Personnel Director
6. Manager
7. Leader

The size, scope, and details of the role may differ from company to company, and the number of people filling each role is greater in larger businesses, but you'll find the same seven roles performed in any successful company in the world. Any job title in any company is simply a variation on one these seven roles.

To get a better understanding of exactly why these roles are so critical, let's take a quick look at each one.

Producer

The producer is the person who actually creates the product or performs the service your company is selling. Odds are, you were a producer in your last job, at least at some point. The producer job often carries with it a lot of job satisfaction, but not typically a lot of money, freedom, or power.

That changes when you start your own business. In the beginning, of course, you're obviously the producer. As you grow, however, you may add additional people to increase your capacity. And in time you may find that you lose the producer role altogether as your other duties take up all of your time and attention.

Therein lies the irony. You've probably chosen to start a home-based business because you love what you do. You're skilled at what you produce and you're looking forward to doing it with more freedom than you've ever had before. But the producer role is only a tiny part of running a home-based business. Being skilled, talented, or creative as a producer by *no means* guarantees you success—because merely being a producer (no matter how good you are) is not enough. Every other role must also be effectively filled. If any of them are lacking, your business will almost surely fail. Bev's first home-based business, a ceramics studio, failed after two years because she only knew how to wear the hat of the producer. She knew nothing about wearing the other hats.

Marketer

"Build a better mousetrap and the world will beat a path to your door." Garbage. Many superior products and services have died in the marketplace while mediocre and even lousy offerings have succeeded. The difference? Marketing. People can't be expected to buy your incredible mousetrap if they don't know about it, now can they?

The marketer is responsible for informing the marketplace about the existence and desirability of your product or service. A great marketer understands all the elements of effective marketing: branding, positioning, copywriting, design, market research, publicity, targeting, pricing, packaging, and human psychology.

Effective marketing is crucial to the success of any product or service. The marketplace is more crowded than ever before. Consumers and business purchasers alike face more choices in more categories than they've ever had. While this is a boon for them, it's a challenge for you. You have to compete for their attention and make a case that what you offer is better for them than any of their other options. Then, and only then, will they beat a path to your door.

Salesperson

Even if people are, in fact, beating the aforementioned path to your door, there's no guarantee that they'll leave with your product or service. Effective marketing gets a prospect to *consider* buying from you. It's the salesperson's job to turn that mere consideration into a buying decision.

Many home business owners are adept at generating interest in what they offer. But because they've never held a selling position, they stumble at transforming that interest into a sale. Selling is not simply putting your product or service in front of a prospect and hoping they'll buy it. It involves actively working to persuade the potential customer that your offering is the right one for them and that now is the right time to buy.

Unfortunately, too many home-business owners are uncomfortable with selling, although their discomfort is understandable. Think of the common stereotype of the salesperson. What descriptive words come to your mind? Perhaps slimy, underhanded, pushy, insincere, even dishonest?

None of us wants to be thought of this way. So we avoid any behavior that we think even *remotely* resembles the stereotype. But sales is a noble and essential profession. Business would grind to a halt without salespeople. And most salespeople are nothing like the stereotype. Instead, they're honest, friendly, and caring. Just as you'll be when you're selling your offerings.

Accountant

The producer, marketer, and salesperson make things happen. The accountant keeps track of what happened. Just because the accountant doesn't bring in revenue, however, doesn't mean the role is any less important. Think what would happen if your clients didn't pay you. Or only paid part of what they owed you. Then think what would happen if your suppliers didn't get paid. Or, worse yet, if your taxes didn't get paid.

The accountant is responsible for maintaining the financial health of your business. This includes billing and collections (accounts receivable), expenses and payroll (accounts payable), and tax preparation and filing (accounts detestable). A good accountant also helps you manage cash flow, minimize taxes and expenses, and plan long-term growth.

Personnel Director

The strength of any business lies in its people. And the smaller a business is, the less margin for error when it comes to choosing people to be part of it. This makes the personnel director's role a crucial one in any business, but especially yours. Even if you expect to be the only employee of your company, you will, at some point, need to outsource certain functions, hire temporary workers or contractors, or even bring in an intern.

The job of the personnel director is to figure out which approach is best and then to select the right person. This includes analyzing the pros and cons of each approach to getting a task accomplished, finding available possibilities, and interviewing candidates. After a person is hired or contracted, the personnel director defines job criteria, monitors their performance, and, if necessary, delivers discipline or termination.

In a home business, a personnel director has additional challenges. Many localities restrict how many employees a home business can have, what kind of work they can do, and even whether they're allowed at all. A good personnel director must be able to meet the labor needs of the business within the restrictions set by local governments and homeowners associations.

Manager

A manager is anyone who has the responsibility of making sure a business's tasks and projects get done. A manager coordinates, plans, monitors, and adjusts. Frequently a manager supervises others, providing assistance, feedback, training, and rewards. A manager is often also an administrator, creating systems for getting things accomplished and administering those systems.

Most people who start home-based businesses find the management aspect to be the biggest shock. The amount of administrative work can seem overwhelming, even for a one-person business. Yet it is work that has to be done if you hope to be successful.

Leader

The terms *leader* and *manager* are often used interchangeably, but they are definitely not the same thing. While a manager can lead and a leader often manages, the two perform very different functions in a company.

In this discussion of the roles in a company, a manager is an operations person, someone who handles the nuts and bolts of a company or a department on a day-to-day basis. A leader, by contrast, focuses on the big picture.

A manager looks at the next few days, weeks, and months. The leader looks at the next 20 years. The leader is the CEO or president, the person who maps out the direction of the company and determines long-term strategy. The leader establishes the philosophy that the company will be governed by, based on his or her goals, priorities, and values.

FILLING THE ROLES

Now that you have a basic idea what each of the roles entails, here's an important point to understand: YOU CAN'T FILL THEM ALL.

No matter how good you are and how independent you want to be, the seven roles require too much time and too many skills for any one person. People who try to do everything inevitably fail, because one or more of the crucial functions doesn't get the skilled attention it deserves.

So now you're starting to worry. One of the reasons you chose to start your own home-based business is because you wanted to be free of people breathing down your neck, screwing up their work, or arguing with you about the best way to do things. You were planning to run your business by yourself and now you're thinking, "How can I possibly succeed on my own if I can't do it all?"

The answer is to get help where you need it. Successful people realize this and delegate. It can even work to your advantage when you delegate tasks to people who are more skilled at them than you are. This doesn't necessarily mean hiring a whole bunch of employees. You can fill all the roles while still remaining a one-person business.

The key is to know which roles you can outsource and how to do it. You can't delegate *everything*, but you can get other people to fill some of the roles productively and cost effectively. Let's look at each of the roles again, and this time examine your options for filling them.

Producer

Whether you can have others work as producers for you depends on two factors: the kind of business you're in and your budget.

If the results your business produces don't depend on specialized or highly skilled labor, it's fairly easy to pay employees or independent contractors to do some or all of the producer work for you. Services like construction, landscaping, catering, delivery, painting, cleaning, and medical billing lend themselves to low-cost, unskilled labor that enable you to do more customer work in less time.

However, if your clients hire you for your particular expertise or talent, that's a different story. For someone like a lawyer, accountant, personal trainer, graphic designer, consultant, or artist, your customer is buying you as much as your product or service. This is not to say that you can't ever hire people to do your producer work, it just takes more time and care. You'll go from simply being a professional to being an owner of a company with a stable of professionals, all of whom produce the same kind of quality work that you do.

The second issue is your budget. Can you afford to hire people to do producer work? As a general rule, producer work is the easiest to pay for because your customers pay for it. This, of course, assumes that you have enough customers to keep your employees or contractors busy. If you're obligated to pay employees but don't have enough revenue to cover their payroll, you have a challenge. And while you generally only have to pay contractors when they're working, if they're *not* working, they won't stay around long.

Marketer

If you read the chapter on marketing your business and still have concerns about your ability to do it effectively, you can relax. While you're the one who is ultimately responsible for your company's marketing, there are several specific marketing functions that you can outsource.

There are a lot of marketing companies out there that can help you figure out an overall company marketing strategy, including a marketing plan, your positioning or niche, a logo, your company color scheme, and more. These companies come in a variety of sizes, experience levels, specialties, and price ranges. Many will do much of the implementing for you, but of course, you pay for that additional service. If you choose to work with such a company, look for one with a proven track record working with companies like yours, and ideally with other home-based businesses.

Another option is to hire companies to do piecemeal marketing work. For example you might hire:

- A graphic designer to create your logo, letterhead, and business cards
- A public relations company to get you media exposure
- An advertising agency to create and place ads for you
- A copywriter to write ad copy and direct mail letters
- A Web design company to build or redo your Web site

As you ponder what to outsource and what to do yourself, weigh the following two ideas: On the one hand, the more you do yourself, the more money you'll save. On the other hand, if you're not skilled in a particular area—graphic design, copywriting, etc.—it's worth the money to pay a professional who will get you better results.

Salesperson

As a business owner, you can't help but be a salesperson. You have to sell your business plan to banks, your services or products to customers, and yourself to almost everyone. You don't have to be the only—or even the primary—salesperson, however. You can hire employees or independent contractors to do some or most of your selling for you.

If you hire other salespeople, it will be up to you to judge their selling skills and their appropriateness for your company and prospects. You will need to teach them what they need to know to sell your goods or services and provide them with sales materials to aid them in their efforts. You'll also need to create a compensation system, monitor their sales activities, and reward or discipline them based on their productivity. In other words, you'll be a sales manager.

Accountant

We have a confession to make: We hate accounting. We detest it with every fiber of our being. We hate recording sales, keeping track of expenses, and doing taxes.

However, we LOVE accountants! We each use an accountant to handle the more maddening aspects of our business finances. And our accountants make a world of difference for us.

Unless you yourself *are* an accountant, it is essential that you retain the services of one. Accounting is too critical a function to leave to chance. Tax laws are too numerous, too complex, and change too frequently for you to keep on top of. A good accountant quickly pays for him- or herself with the money they save you, not to mention the headaches they relieve you of.

You don't need to have an accountant on staff or even on retainer. You can work with an accountant on an as-needed basis, although you should meet with yours at least once a quarter.

Personnel Director

When you start your company, you're the only employee. You can set your own work rules, decide how much and when you get paid, and judge your results for yourself. And you can do it all without writing anything down.

But as soon as you need to get someone else involved in the business, whether it's a family member, an employee, an intern, or a contractor, everything changes. You take on the responsibilities of a personnel director.

If you have no experience as a personnel director, you can get assistance. You can get referrals to service professionals for work you want to outsource. You can purchase standardized paperwork and forms. You can even use temp agencies and staffing services to find potential employees who are prescreened.

Nonetheless, the final decisions about who to hire, what to pay them, and whether they should be rewarded or terminated rests with you. The selection and care of the people who make up your company is one of your greatest responsibilities.

Manager

For many home-based entrepreneurs, the day-to-day office and business management tasks are the least favorite parts of their business. Fortunately, it's fairly easy to hire an administrative assistant or an office manager to take over some or all of your administrative work. The more you need done for you, the more experienced the person you'll need to hire—and the more you'll have to pay. It's money well spent, though. Letting someone else handle your "busywork" frees you up to do what you do best, making the best use of your time.

Keep in mind that you will still be this person's manager. You'll need to give instructions, guidance, and feedback. At the same time, ask for ideas, insights, and feedback. An office manager, an administrative assistant, or even an intern can be a valuable resource as a fresh pair of eyes and a different perspective.

Leader

Since your company is your idea, it's unlikely you will ever give up the role of the leader. That doesn't mean you can't get help with what a leader must do. You might not have a clue as to what direction you should take your business. Or you might not be skilled in planning long-term strategy.

If that's the case, you can get assistance from a mentor, a coach, or a consultant. Such a person should be someone with considerable business experience, and someone you respect and trust. One resource for business mentors is the Service Corps of Retired Executives (SCORE), which you can learn more about from your local Small Business Development Center (SBDC). Check also with your local Office of Economic Development or Chamber of Commerce to see if a business mentor program is available in your area.

WORKING WITH OTHERS

The above discussion has been predicated on the assumption that you're planning to run your business by yourself, at least for the foreseeable future. But if you plan to go into business with a spouse, a relative, or some other partner, you have a completely different situation, one with a big advantage and a big challenge.

The advantage is that there are two of you (or more). Which means more labor, more brainpower, and more variety of perspective. It also means that each person can take on some of the roles, relieving the other of having to do so much.

The challenge is that anytime there's more than one person involved in a business, there is potential for conflict. Some conflict is normal for a business, and even healthy, but too much can doom it to failure. To avoid this fate, it's critical for you and everyone else you're going into business with to sit down ahead of time and agree upon:

- The company vision
- Who will take what roles
- How each person will treat the others
- Specific areas of responsibility
- Levels of authority
- Company hierarchy
- Decision-making processes
- Conflict-resolution procedures

Settling these issues beforehand will prevent many conflicts from occurring and will make those that do crop up easier to resolve. This is especially important in a home-based business, where relationships are already highly emotional and you may have to live with the people you work with.

BUSINESS-BUILDING SKILLS

Operating a successful home-based business requires a lot of skill. And a lot of *skills*. Each of the roles we've discussed involves a number of unique skills. Taken together, they are a laundry list of what you need to make your business thrive. They also illustrate why so many home-based businesses fail—not because of a lack of talent or passion, but because of a lack of business-building skills.

Take a look at the "Business Skills Checklist" on the next page and mark the skills that you think you're already competent in. The remaining items will give you a sense of what you need to improve or outsource in order for you to succeed.

Don't ignore any of them. Each and every one is needed in your business. In examining each skill, we'll briefly discuss its importance and how you can improve your competence in it.

Accounting

Hopefully by now we've persuaded you to hire an accountant to help you with your financial management, record keeping, and tax preparation. This doesn't let you entirely off the hook, however. You still need to have a fundamental grasp of the basic principles of accounting to understand what your accountant is telling you.

You also need to keep an eye on the financial health of your business, which means reviewing your books, checking your balance sheet, and examining your profit and loss statements. If your business is in trouble, it's better to know that sooner rather than later.

Computers and Technology

You don't have to be a technogeek, but you can't afford to be a technophobe either. While it's possible today to run a business without good computer skills, it's not an efficient, effective, or profitable way. The computer is arguably the most important business tool ever invented, and if you don't know how to effectively unleash its power, you're missing incredible opportunities.

BUSINESS SKILLS CHECKLIST

❏ Accounting

❏ Computer
   and Technology

❏ Conflict Resolution

❏ Crisis Management

❏ Decision Making

❏ Design

❏ Filing

❏ Interviewing

❏ Management

❏ Marketing

❏ Negotiating

❏ Networking

❏ People

❏ Planning

❏ Project
   Management

❏ Selling

❏ Speaking

❏ Time Management

❏ Typing

❏ Writing

At the very least you should know how to operate the basic software programs you need to run your business: word processor, spreadsheet, contact manager, e-mail, and so on. You can take a class in any major software program from many adult education programs, community colleges, public seminar companies, and computer retailers. There are also home-study courses on video and CD-ROM available by mail order, not to mention myriad books written for everyone from first-time computer users to near-experts. (*Note:* We're not counting the "manuals" that actually come with the software, most of which seem to have been written by drunken walruses.)

You also need to know a little about the hardware, operating system, and peripherals so you can perform preventive maintenance and troubleshoot when things go wrong. The more problems you can solve yourself, the better. Dealing with virtually any company's tech support can be expensive, frustrating, and time-consuming.

Conflict Resolution

If human beings are involved, conflicts are going to happen. You can't prevent them all and you can't ignore them. So how will you handle them? Giving in all the time is not practical, and neither is always demanding that you get your way.

There has been a lot of work done over the past few years on the subject of conflict resolution, and as a result, there are a number of new books, seminars, and audio programs available. Don't argue with us, just invest in one.

Crisis Management

Things don't always go smoothly in business, and often when they go wrong, they do so at the worst possible time. The fact that your business is home-based increases the number of crises that can possibly occur: You don't have to worry just about business crises, you have to worry about home and family crises as well.

You can't anticipate everything that might go wrong. But you can prepare yourself and learn what to do when common crises occur. Being able to stay calm and come up with a plan is the first step in dealing with any crisis.

Decision Making

When you're an employee, you often don't have much decision-making authority. But as the business owner, every decision is yours. While you can't expect to make the best possible decision every time, you *can* learn to improve your decision-making skills overall. Decision making is a science, and new research is demonstrating that it's an art as well. There are some books available on the subject, but business magazines are where you'll find the latest insights in this new field.

Design

Good graphic design is essential for a business and it's probably the hardest thing on this list to teach. If you're not naturally artistic, it's going to be far more efficient and cost effective to simply have a design professional do all your design work for you.

Having said that, however, we should point out that you have the final say in all design issues. If you love what your designer has created, great. If *don't* love it, stop and hold everything. Ask your designer why she thinks what she's produced will be effective for you. If you're still unconvinced, solicit the opinions of friends and other business owners. And you can always consult with another designer to get a second professional opinion.

Filing

Don't laugh. Filing is not as unimportant as it sounds. The average businessperson wastes 10 hours a week looking for misplaced items in their office. That's time you could much better spend on more productive activities.

Searching through clutter also increases your stress level. Heck, just *looking* at clutter all day can increase your stress level. Which will only rise as you discover missed deadlines, forgotten payments, and lost opportunities due to an unorganized office.

Creating a practical and efficient filing system takes considerable organizational skills. If you're "organizationally challenged" (as many of us are), hire an organization expert who can create filing systems and teach you how to use them effectively.

Interviewing

Because you have to be the personnel director (lucky you), it's critical for you to be a good interviewer. Even if you don't plan to hire employees or contractors, you'll need sharp interviewing skills to determine which lawyer, accountant, graphic designer, etc., is best for you.

And if you do plan to hire employees, it's crucial that you know and understand the laws that pertain to hiring. There are many questions you're not allowed by law to ask during an interview. Determining whether a job candidate is suitable without asking any illegal questions takes considerable effort.

Management

Management is a discipline unto itself, which is why so many first-time managers find themselves confused and frustrated. It's also a much-researched and debated discipline, which is why there are so many books on the subject, many of which conflict with one another.

Whether you'll be working alone or with others, you need to learn as much about management as you can. Some theories and practices will fit your personality and your business better than others, but almost any knowledge in the field of management will help you. Focus your attention on books that specifically relate to small business management. They'll be more likely to relate to your situation than others.

Marketing

Regardless of how much of the marketing function you outsource, you need a fundamental understanding of what marketing is and how it works. You also need to make sure that your business is marketing consistently and that the marketing you're doing is working. The more you learn about marketing and the more actively involved you are in it, the better for your business.

Negotiating

You negotiate with almost everyone you come into contact with, from suppliers and clients to airlines and credit card companies to your spouse and kids. Being able to negotiate effectively means you'll get more of what you want, more of the time. It also means your counterpart will be more satisfied with the outcome. Time and money spent learning to negotiate better will pay immediate dividends, not just with your business, but in virtually every area of your life.

Networking

The larger your Rolodex, the more resources you have at your disposal. Although it's not just who you know, but who knows *you*. And *likes* you. The time to make a friend is long before you need one.

We will briefly discuss networking when we go into marketing in Chapter 10, "Getting the World to Beat a Path to Your Door." But we barely scratch the surface, and networking is more than just about marketing. Through networking, you can find vendors, employees, business partners, and more.

Networking is also valuable as a social outlet. For many home-based business owners, networking is an opportunity to get out of the house and have a conversation with someone other than the kids. (Or the dog!)

So if you avoid networking because you get nervous in a room full of strangers, take comfort in the fact that Don used to be painfully shy and now is a leading authority on networking! If he can learn to be an effective networker, so can you.

People

Because so many aspects of business are tied to relationships and interaction with others, a "people person" has a distinct advantage. Social skills are not formally taught in schools, but they're of supreme importance in the real world. Every encounter you have with a prospect, customer, supplier, colleague, journalist, or anyone else leaves them with an impression of you. If that impression is negative, you're in trouble.

That may not be any fault of your own. You may just be uncomfortable or awkward in social situations. Or you may be less sensitive to other people's feelings than most people. Or you may have some annoying habit that you're not even aware of. You may turn people off without knowing you have a problem.

Fortunately, you can improve your social skills if you're not naturally a people person. First, talk with those closest to you to get an appraisal of your people skills. Awareness is the first step. Then learn more about whatever your weakness is. People will react and relate to you more positively.

Planning

A successful home-based business doesn't just happen. It requires a tremendous amount of planning. As we discussed in Chapter 4, "Mapping Out Your Route to Success," you'll need to write a business plan before you even get your business started. And included in your business plan will be a marketing plan, financial plan, and family plan.

Once your business plan is written, however, don't think you're done. As you progress with your business, you're going to be creating monthly plans, yearly plans, and five-year plans. You're also going to need to review your business plan and revise parts of it on a regular basis.

Project Management

Making a project come together by its deadline requires planning, coordination, follow-up, and an ability to adjust. Project management is truly a skill unto itself. If you don't have experience as a project manager, take a class or seminar in project management. You'll appreciate it when you complete your first project.

Selling

The more skilled you are at selling, the more sales you'll make. If you're not an experienced salesperson or you're not comfortable with the idea of selling, read a book, listen to an audio program, or take a class or seminar before you even start your business.

If you do have experience selling, don't rest on your laurels. You can never learn too much about selling. There are always new ideas, new approaches, and new tools. And relearning stuff you've forgotten can be just as valuable as learning new ideas. The best salespeople are always studying more about sales. That's why they're the best.

Speaking

Getting your point across verbally is required of you almost daily. Whether you're making a sales presentation to a prospective client, pitching your company to possible investors, or delivering your 60-second commercial in front of your local Chamber of Commerce, knowing how to effectively speak in front of a group can make the difference between a stunning success and a cataclysmic failure.

To ensure the former rather than the latter, brush up on your oral communication skills. Take a class in public speaking through your local adult education program or community college. Or join Toastmasters International, a nonprofit organization that helps people in all walks of life to develop their speaking skills in a friendly, supportive environment. Visit their Web site (www.toastmasters.org) to find a chapter near you.

Time Management

In the next chapter, "Managing Your Time, Your Life, and Your Sanity," we'll go into time management. For now, suffice it to say that with everything you'll be responsible for, managing your time will be more critical to your success than ever before. You'll also have to balance your time between business and family, a real challenge when your office is only a few steps away from your living room.

Typing

You don't have to be an 80-words-per-minute keyboard whiz, but you should at least be a competent touch-typist. Creating documents takes so much longer if you have to use the two finger hunt-and-peck method. If your typing skills are slowing you down, buy a software program that will teach you how to type faster.

If you absolutely hate typing and don't even want to learn, there is an alternative. Voice recognition software enables you to talk to your computer and have your words appear as text on the screen. It takes a while for you and the software to figure out how to work together (you have to "train" the software to understand the way you speak), but it will make you more productive.

Writing

Written communication skills are essential for any business owner. Even if you outsource your copywriting, you still have to write letters, contracts, e-mails, proposals, and more. And you can't rely on spelling and grammar checkers in your word processor to make your writing understandable.

If you don't already have excellent writing skills, take a class or a seminar on business writing. Unlike a standard writing class, you'll focus on the kinds of written communications you have to deal with on a regular basis.

WHEW!

If this list seems overwhelming, you're right. It is. Welcome to the world of being your own boss. The key is to focus on your strengths and get help for the areas in which you're weaker. The more work you can turn over to others, the more time and effort you can spend on the activities you do best and enjoy most.

Nobody said it would be easy. In fact, starting your own business will likely be the most difficult project you've ever undertaken. But if you prepare yourself and plan accordingly, it will likely also be the most rewarding.

Chapter 9

MANAGING YOUR TIME, YOUR LIFE, AND YOUR SANITY

How to Get (Almost) Everything Done without Going Crazy

One of the most important factors for home-based business owners is the blending of personal and business life. Remember, you are not just operating a business from your home—you're creating a new lifestyle for yourself. The challenges associated with a home-based business are magnified when it comes to time management. The techniques remain virtually the same, but the business clock at home is based on 24 hours, not the traditional nine-to-five (although even in the non-home-based business, nine-to-five no longer is traditional either).

In order to make the most of your personal and professional time, it's important to know what you want to achieve with the time you have available. Take into account the fact that you are living and working under the same roof. You'll want to integrate your personal life into your business life and vice versa. Unexpected things happen in life, and having good time management skills as well as delegation skills will allow you to balance work and family under the same roof.

Bev has handled numerous time management challenges in her home-based business life. One of them occurred when her mother-in-law, Eva, was diagnosed with pancreatic cancer. Once the doctors determined there was nothing they could do for her, she was moved into the Williams household with hospice care. The room across the hall from Bev's office was converted into a hospital room.

The challenge became managing her business and a terminally ill family member. Once a routine was established, Bev found that there were many things Eva could do—and was more than willing to do—to help the business. She became a sounding board, a proofreader, and an envelope stuffer. Clients were understanding, and in fact began visiting Eva when they came to the office on business. Bev's teenage son, her husband, and other family members and friends helped whenever possible. Time management skills made it possible to give a terminally ill family member quality attention for eight months, and for Bev to continue her business at the same time.

SET GOALS

Set long-term goals for your personal life and your business. Be certain that the goals reflect your values and priorities, not a friend's, a consultant's, or a book author's. They need to originate from you. Make sure they are measurable, attainable, and specific so you can manage your progress on a day-to-day basis. What does that mean?

One of Bev's first goals in her desktop publishing business was to have enough clients to make a profit. That wasn't a very measurable or specific goal. She then had to decide how many clients or client projects she would need in order to cover her business expenses and have money left over. It became clear that not all of her clients could be newsletter clients since all of them would have deadlines about the same time. She needed other types of client work to fill in the other days of the month. Some clients were long-term clients, and others were occasional or onetime clients. Once it was determined how many of each she needed, those numbers were worked into her marketing plan and her goals were set. These goals were now measurable, attainable, and specific.

For personal goals, it was important to Bev to spend time with her family, especially a grandchild who lived nearby, as well as to have time to do crafts. Because she did her best work in the morning, she often spent five or six hours in the office, then took a few hours off in the afternoon to take her grandson to the playground. She would then go back into the office in the late afternoon or evening to work if necessary. The time away from the office renewed her energy and allowed creative ideas to jell in her mind.

Don's goals, however, are very different. As a sales and marketing expert who speaks professionally, his business goals relate to the number of speaking engagements per year, type of engagements, and number and type of clients. He also sets goals for creating new books, audio programs, and other learning tools.

Being single, Don's personal goals are also very different from Bev's. His nonwork priorities focus on friends, dating, and recreation. (At least when he's not traveling like crazy.) He's also very active in his local chapter of the National Speakers Association and his local Chamber of Commerce.

So what you need to decide is, what are *your* priorities? What do you want to do in your business and personal life? What will it take for both of them to be successful? How do you even *define* success? Once you've determined your personal and professional goals, you can begin to create systems to help you achieve them.

GET ORGANIZED

In order to be organized and accomplish the important items in your personal and professional life, you need specific tools for managing yourself, such as a personal organizer, a computer, and sufficient work and file space. In most home offices, space is at a premium, and clutter can slow you down dramatically. If you can't find what you need, when you need it, you're losing valuable time. Investing a few hours doing some systematic filing will pay for itself almost immediately in increased efficiency. File everything you absolutely need to keep and throw out what you don't need.

Get a contact manager software program or a day planner to keep track of names, numbers, and other critical information. If you use a cell phone, consider keeping important numbers and memos in the cell phone so that when you're on the road, you don't need to carry a planner and your cell phone with you.

Get into the habit of keeping a phone log or at least a pad of paper near your phone to jot down notes, phone numbers, etc. Don't use scrap pieces of paper that will get lost before you can blink an eye. Consider writing phone numbers, e-mail addresses, addresses, etc. on the inside of a client file folder (and/or staple their business card to the inside of the folder). If you then keep the client file in the proper place, you'll always be able to find the contact information.

For your business, focus on projects that you know will provide long-term benefits. Decide what constitutes a good day's work for you. (Be sure to read the next chapter, about marketing. Marketing is an ongoing business project that needs careful planning.) These are activities and programs that will help your business both today and tomorrow. If you are focused on the desired outcome, your efforts will not be wasted. The impact of your focus will be the ability to control activities and events that are unscheduled but important to you and your business.

To-Do Lists

Make a to-do list daily. Actually, it should be a "done" list since the challenge is to assemble your list on a daily basis with a commitment to actually getting it done on the date for which the list appears. The best time to plan the to-do list is at the end of the day, enabling you to make your priority commitments when you're least likely to be interrupted. Make a big deal out of crossing off the items as you accomplish the "to-dos."

Concentrate your activities on one thing at a time. You will only be able to do this if your work space and mind are free from clutter. A cluttered work space makes concentration difficult, if not impossible. You'll always find an excuse not to work on your most important activity if you're constantly distracted by clutter. The ability to focus on the important tasks will result in your best productivity and profit for your business. Spend a few minutes every day filing and organizing your office. It's easier to handle a few things at a time than wait until the piles are a foot high. It then becomes an overwhelming task that seems to take forever and interrupts your work flow.

Delegate everything you can to others. Sounds difficult, especially when you're working from your home. The reality is, you have several choices for delegation. Delegate personal responsibilities to others in your household. This may be the time to have children learn homemaking skills such as laundry and cooking.

Family members can also help in the business. Age-appropriate tasks such as filing, copying, envelope stuffing, and stamping can be done by just about anyone. Asking your family members for help in both personal and business tasks can free you to do the things for your business that only you can do. Family involvement in your business will result in an understanding of your business efforts and a feeling of pride and cooperation, instead of complaints that you're physically there but not there for them in other ways.

If you live by yourself, decide what's important to you. If having a spotless house is important, consider hiring a cleaning service once or twice a month to do the heavy cleaning. Schedule daily household tasks into your to-do list. Mowing the grass or washing your car can be a break from your work and provide renewed energy.

For your business needs, you may want to hire people capable of doing the professional tasks you don't enjoy doing. For instance, unless your business is designing marketing materials, you might want to consider hiring someone else to design yours. Other tasks that could be outsourced include accounting, deliveries, collections, writing, or editing. It is not a good use of your time to tackle these things if they aren't part of your skills. If cash flow is a problem, consider trading services with another home-based business owner. They may be in the same spot you are and would appreciate the opportunity to trade services. (See Chapter 14, "Employees or Independent Contractors?" for information on hiring others to help in your business.)

Set up "availability hours" and "quiet time." This is not only for your benefit, but your family's and clients' sake as well. Consider blocking out 11 a.m. to 12 noon daily to return calls—make this message known on your voice mail. The perception to people you do business with is that you are busy—this will have lasting value to your business relationships. And if your family is given a specific time as to your availability, their perception of you will be beneficial as well—they'll respect your work hours.

During quiet time, turn off the ringer on your business and personal phone, and turn the volume on your answering machine, if you have one, to the lowest setting. You will be able to work better without the interruptions, and can return calls after you've finished your work. If you're the type that can't ignore the telephone, at least monitor your calls. This is one advantage to having an answering machine in your office rather than using a voice mail service. However, you can do the same thing with voice mail by simply letting the service answer the call and then call to find out who left you a message. Personally, we encourage you to simply turn off all sound so you can give your full attention to the work you need to do. There is rarely something so important that it can't wait an hour or two.

Consider making an A and a B to-do list. The A list is what absolutely must be accomplished that day—both professionally and personally. The B list consists of tasks or chores you would like to accomplish if time allows. Cross off each item as you accomplish it. Use colored pencils to cross through the item or totally obliterate it with bold, wide strokes. There is such satisfaction in looking at this list both periodically and at the end of the day and seeing those crossed off items.

Do it now. Don't waste time procrastinating. Focus on what needs to get done, be sure you know why it's important, and JUST DO IT!

FORGING A BALANCE
Learn to Say No
Learn to say no constructively. The trick here is for you to learn to be comfortable with not having to say yes to every request that comes your way personally and professionally. Saying no is certainly a challenge, but the impact on your time will be favorable. If said in a way that communicates courtesy and respect, the results on your business will be favorable as well.

Remember not to plan more than 60 percent of your day. This will allow you plenty of time for adjustments resulting from interruptions or crises. You can always fill in free time with other tasks, personal or professional. However, if you schedule 100 percent of your time, you will find it impossible to truly accomplish your goals.

Time On and Off
Give yourself time off as a special reward when you've accomplished important tasks or objectives. You will need to be the first person to pat yourself on the back. Remember that you're the boss, the owner, the CEO. There is no one else to turn to for the little things that someone else may have given you praise for when working for someone else.

Take time off, even if it's for an hour or two. Being able to take a break during the middle of a workday is one of the biggest perks of working at home. These breaks can reduce your stress and increase your personal satisfaction. So go ahead, read a book, watch a movie, or have coffee with a friend. Going for a walk around the neighborhood or spending some time working in your garden can be good for your body and your mind.

Your break activity could even be business related, such as spending time to research a new piece of equipment for your business. You need relaxation, and if you can tie it to accomplishing something in your business, then you'll gain the sense of achievement and greater self-esteem needed to go on to the next major task or activity.

Don't forget to schedule vacation time. You may not be able or willing to take the length of vacation time you did when employed by corporate America, but you can and should take enough time away from the business to enjoy the fruits of your labors.

If you travel as part of your business, consider extending your travel to visit nearby areas. Family members can often accompany you on business trips with little extra cost. As a frequent traveler, Don makes it a point to schedule time with friends and family in the cities he visits whenever he has the opportunity.

Listen to Your Body

Our internal clocks dictate our ability to be productive. Do your most challenging tasks when your mind and body are at their peak. For example, Don is a night person, so he takes advantage of his schedule flexibility by frequently working past midnight and then sleeping in until nine or so most mornings. Bev, on the other hand, is a morning person who works best between 8 a.m. and 2 p.m., then goes on to other personal tasks. She will sometimes return to her office in the evening for a few more hours.

Break Up Your Workday

As professional speakers, we both often have engagements in the evening, so we will exercise, meet with friends, or run errands during the morning or afternoon. We still put in 8 to 10 hours a day on business, just not consecutively.

Don has a friend who typically starts her workday at 6 a.m. and goes until 6 p.m., but she schedules three or four hours during that time to run errands, write in her journal, and go running or hiking. As your own boss, you can break up your workday however it works best for you.

Keep a Log

It's easy to feel guilty about not working "normal" business hours. You may need to give yourself permission to work according to your own schedule. If this is a problem for you, try keeping a log of your day. Record, in half-hour or 15-minute increments, how you are spending your time over the course of a day or a week. If you see on paper that your total time spent working is what it should be, you'll feel more comfortable with your newfound flexibility.

Go Cordless

Being chained to your desk is a terrible waste of a bright, sunny day. Using portable tools of the trade will let you enjoy the freedom that you started a home-based business for in the first place. With a laptop computer (or even a notepad and pen) and a cordless phone you can work al fresco. Grab a cell phone and a wireless modem and you can stay plugged in while getting away from it all. Take your kids to the lake or the park and let them run and shout while you run spreadsheets.

Find Your Own Style

Some people enjoy blending their business life with their family life. They make the most of their time by multitasking: doing laundry while printing out documents, helping with homework while preparing a mailing, and so on. Other people need to keep their business and family lives strictly separated. They work most efficiently by focusing on one thing at a time. The better approach is the one that works more effectively for you. Once you've figured out how you work best, let our family know so they can work with you rather than against you.

ENJOYING THE HOLIDAYS

Chestnuts roasting on an open fire, Jack Frost nipping at your nose, and Santa Claus coming to town usually summon warm thoughts about the coming holidays. Whatever holidays you celebrate—Chanukah, Kwanzaa, Christmas, Ramadan—they can be extremely stressful even though we all look forward to them. For home-based business owners, it can bring on a case of the Home Office Holiday Horrors! Here are some strategies for enjoying the holidays without sacrificing work.

Be Realistic

When you are already working more than 40 hours per week, adding holiday shopping and entertaining can bust your time budget. Use the ABC method of prioritizing to manage your responsibilities and expectations: A being the most important, like sending out your invoices and meeting client deadlines; and C being least imperative, such as decorating the house.

Hold On to Your Money

If you've been thinking of upgrading or buying a new piece of office equipment, look for holiday sales. Buying before the end of the year means you can use the expense to reduce your taxable income.

Buy holiday cards after the holidays or during the spring or summer. Address them at your leisure while on the phone or while you're waiting for someone.

Instead of spending days running around town doing your annual holiday shopping, get some mail order catalogs. Browse through them while sipping your morning coffee, eating lunch, or watching TV in the evening. Most mail order catalog companies also have secure Web sites for ordering online. Some even offer free shipping with a minimum purchase.

Make your own gifts. You don't have to be crafty. Try putting together a gift in a jar. There are numerous books with lots of recipes. Bev does this for her customers and friends with a personalized tag attached that is printed with her own printer. Or bake a batch of cookies or make some candy. Don makes chocolate truffles every year and puts them in inexpensive plastic containers. These types of gifts are greatly appreciated by clients and friends, and you may find your family will be happy to help save you even more time by pitching in.

Consider writing an end-of-the-year letter to your top clients—or all of them, if you're not overloaded—thanking them for helping you make this a successful year for your business. Announce any new products or services you will be adding in the next year, and maybe even offer a "thank you" discount for the next time they need your service or product.

Decorate Your Office

Add some holiday cheer to your work environment by sprucing up your office with greeting cards addressed to your business. Add some appropriate decorations for the holiday to your window or door. An aesthetically pleasing work space is a motivating mood booster.

Do Something Charitable

Donate a food basket or provide a service to a charitable organization in the name of your business. Volunteer a few hours of your time or even write a check. You'll feel good and you'll be giving something back to the community.

Avoid Isolation and Have Some Fun

Invite your clients to an informal open house at your office (if you have room). Today's trend to live and work under the same roof tends to isolate us from face-to-face contact with our clients. If they don't normally come to your office, they might appreciate the opportunity to see where you work.

If clients invite you to their holiday celebrations, give yourself a time limit. Spend enough time with them to be social (it's good for building strong relationships), but get back to your own work as soon as possible.

If you have never dealt with time management before or feel you're not good at it, consider taking a seminar or reading up on the subject. There are several good time management books available.

Your business is important, but so is the rest of your life. These ideas will help the two coexist more peacefully. Keep in mind that your specific priorities will change from day to day and week to week. The important thing is to aim for an overall balance in your life and to appreciate the little things. Like a bright, sunny day.

Chapter 10

GETTING THE WORLD TO BEAT A PATH TO YOUR DOOR

How to Market Your Business without a Huge Budget

As a home-based business owner, you have several unique challenges when it comes to marketing your products and services. You don't have a storefront. You can't put up an eight-foot sign outside your office. And if you're like most home-based businesspeople, you don't have much of an advertising budget.

Yet marketing is one of the most crucial tasks you need to undertake if your business is to survive, much less grow. The biggest reason most home businesses fail is a lack of customers due to insufficient—or nonexistent—marketing.

So how can you alert potential customers to your business without breaking the bank? The answer is to look at marketing in a new way. Don't think just in terms of advertisements in newspapers, magazines, and the yellow pages, or commercials on radio and TV. Because marketing is everything you do to promote your business, from the name of your company to the way you dress when you meet the public to your policies for resolving customer complaints.

If marketing seems overwhelming and complicated, relax—it's not. You don't need a marketing degree to effectively market your business. You *do* need a willingness to try new things, and you need a commitment to devote time and energy on a regular, consistent basis to your marketing efforts.

In this chapter we'll share with you dozens of free and low-cost marketing tactics you can use to promote your business. Most of them you can do yourself, right in your home. Choose several to start with and add one or two on a regular basis, because the more you use, the better your sales will be.

PRINT MATERIALS

Effective print materials require great graphic design. Unless you yourself are a graphic designer, you'll want to hire a professional to create or redo the graphic image of your business. While it may seem a considerable expense, it's really an investment. Good graphic design gives your stationery, business cards, brochures, fax cover sheets, and other printed materials a consistent, professional look and can last you for many years.

Predesigned stationery, available at office supply stores and through mail-order catalogs, may seem a cost-effective alternative, but they can work against you. First, the paper quality may be poor, especially business card stock. Second, you run the risk of the "popularity paradox": If the design you pick isn't popular, the manufacturer may discontinue it, forcing you to change your entire graphic image. On the other hand, if the design *is* popular, it means that thousands of other people are using it as well, which can result in your prospects getting letters and business cards from other businesses that look just like yours.

Business Cards

Your business card is your most fundamental marketing piece. You give it out to everyone you meet and you include it with your correspondence. It is what people will use to remember you and to contact you. Here are some guidelines to making your card as effective as possible:

- Give your card a good look and feel. Splurge on the paper. Cheap, flimsy paper says "cheap, flimsy company." Use the thickest, nicest paper you can afford. It's one of your cheapest upgrades.
- Remember the power of color. It makes your business more professional and memorable. Either your paper or your ink (preferably both) should be in at least one of your corporate colors. If you don't have any corporate colors, talk with a marketing consultant or graphic designer with a specialty in marketing. Color printing costs only a little more than black and white, with a tremendous difference in the impact. And four-color printing can be surprisingly affordable.
- Adding a picture, a graphic, or your logo to your card makes it more visually appealing and aids memory retention. The most powerful

graphic you can use is your own picture, because it gives a human face to your business. And we all remember faces better than names.
- Make it easy for your potential customers to contact you. Your card should list all the ways of getting in touch with you, including your address or P.O. box (but not both, to avoid confusion), office phone, cell phone, fax number (all with area code), e-mail address, and Web site.

You can even add more information and turn your business card into a mini brochure. You might include your days and hours of operation, brands you carry, services you offer, a map, helpful tips, or anything else you can think of that would be helpful to your customer. Remember, however, that your type size should always be 8 points or larger to ensure easy readability. So, where do you put all this extra information? The back of the card, an extremely valuable yet commonly overlooked piece of marketing real estate.

Keep in mind that whenever any of your contact information changes, you want to get new cards printed immediately. Using labels or a stamp to add the new information to your old cards costs nearly as much and looks far less professional.

Brochures

Brochures are the Swiss army knife of marketing materials. A good brochure serves many functions. You can leave them in literature racks at Chambers of Commerce and other local organizations. You can hand them out at trade shows, craft fairs, and networking events. You can mail them as either a follow-up or a direct mail piece.

A brochure gives you room to tell your story, in both words and pictures. It provides you with an opportunity to make the case to your prospect why they should buy from you. And if creativity is part of what you're selling, a brochure serves as a canvas for you to show your stuff.

The cost can be anywhere from virtually nothing to thousands of dollars. A brochure can be fashioned from one sheet of ordinary 8½-by-11-inch copy paper or from multipage glossy card stock. You can design and print your brochure yourself on your own computer with desktop publishing software and a good color printer. This allows you to update it as needed or wanted. Or you can have your brochure written, laid out, and printed professionally. Or you can do something in between. Whatever approach you choose depends on several factors, including:

- Your budget
- The image you want to project
- Your target market and their expectations
- The quantity you need
- How long you expect to use the brochure

Whatever the size and shape of your brochure, you want to pack it with information that will help your prospects decide to buy from you. Here are some items you should consider including:

- Testimonials
- Reviews
- Complete listing of products or services
- Credentials and experience
- Awards you've won
- What makes you unique
- Photos
- Products or services
- You and your employees
- Customers
- Before and after shots
- Prices
- Map and/or directions
- Days and hours of operation
- Full contact information
- Your Web site and what they'll find there
- Coupon or special offer for first-time customers

You can increase the chances that your prospect will keep your brochure by turning it into a reference piece. Add some phone numbers for related organizations, helpful tips and guidelines, or Web sites that your prospect might find of interest. If your brochure is useful, it won't get thrown away.

Flyers

Like brochures, flyers are extremely flexible. They can be mailed out, handed out, or left in a rack. In addition, they can be posted on bulletin boards, taped to telephone poles, or slipped underneath windshield wipers. You can use them for individual products or services, package deals, or your business in general.

Flyers are also cost effective. Because they only require one-color printing and the simplest of layouts, you can create them yourself on your computer and photocopy as many as you need.

When creating your flyer, make sure it's got a strong headline that promises a benefit or a solution to a problem. Include as much information about features and benefits as you think is necessary to entice a prospect to call you, e-mail you, or visit your Web site. And, of course, be certain your full contact information is there and easy to find.

To catch the reader's eye, incorporate some kind of visual image, such as a photo or a drawing. Be sure to use colored paper stock to really make your flyers stand out. You can even create flyers in odd sizes or shapes to grab your prospect's attention.

DIRECT MAIL

Direct mail can be a powerful and cost-effective way to reach your prospects. It brings your message right into their office or living room. The trick is to get them to open it and then to move them to action. Putting together an effective direct mail campaign requires planning, effort, knowledge, and at least a little money. The results, however, can be tremendous.

There are four elements that are important for a successful direct mail effort: the mailing list, the message you send, an expiration date, and making it easy to respond to your offer.

The Mailing List The single most important element in a successful direct mail effort is the mailing list. If you send your message to people who aren't interested in what you have to sell, you'll get no response whatsoever. By contrast, if you could send your offer only to people who are interested, your response would be near 100 percent. So the more closely your mailing list matches your target market, the better your results will be.

You can rent mailing lists from Chambers of Commerce, professional associations, magazines, newspapers, government agencies, and list brokers. You can typically request a subset of the full list, determined by any demographic criteria you want. For example, you could ask for just the people on the list who live in a certain geographic area or are in a particular age range or in a specific industry. The more sorting criteria you use, the more expensive the list will be per name. However, you'll save money on both printing and postage, without sacrificing your response rate.

The Message   The next component of an effective direct mail effort is the message. What you say to your prospect in your mailing must intrigue, excite, or amaze them. You need to tap into your prospect's needs, desires, fears, or anxieties. Your marketing message is not so much about you, your service, or your product—it's about how what you sell will benefit your customer.

For example, will your product or service reduce their labor expenses? Will it protect them from legal action? Will it save them time? Will it eliminate a hassle from their life? Will it prevent their computer from crashing? Will it keep their car running longer? Will it let them express their pride in their children?

Your marketing message doesn't need to explain every detail about your product or service. Your prospect is bombarded by enough of those messages every day. What your message *does* need to do is explain how your offering will solve their problem or improve their life.

An Expiration Date   The third key to a fruitful direct mail effort is to make a specific offer with an expiration date. We all have so many things competing for our time that something has to be special to attract our attention. And because of all we have to do, our natural inclination is to put off anything that isn't urgent. So offer your prospects some kind of deal they can't normally get, and include a deadline to create a sense of urgency.

An Easy Response   The fourth element of a successful direct mail piece is to make it easy to respond to your offer. Once you've piqued your prospect's interest, you have to move them to action. And the easier that action is to take, the more likely they will take it. Ideally, you want to give your prospect a variety of ways to respond to you:

- Calling you on the phone (preferably via a toll-free number)
- Faxing a response form
- Mailing back a postage-paid card
- Sending you an e-mail
- Visiting your Web site

Tell your prospect precisely what to do, how and when to do it, and why it will be beneficial to them to do so. Follow the above rules for success with any of the following direct mail tools.

Letters

The most important part of an effective direct mail letter actually has nothing to do with the letter itself. It's the envelope. If the envelope doesn't entice your prospect to open it, the most brilliantly written letter will never get read.

So how do you ensure that the envelope gets opened? The key is to pique the prospects' interest enough to make them spend the time and energy to look at the contents rather than simply tossing it unopened into the trash with the rest of the "junk mail."

One way to entice your prospects is to put something bulky inside the envelope. Small, lightweight items like a pen or a key chain work well. You neither need nor want the object to be huge, just something that creates a bump in the envelope so your prospect wonders, "Hmm, what is this?" A graphic designer in Olney, Maryland, sends out Valentine's Day cards to her clients with a heart-shaped lollipop inside. We doubt anyone throws away that envelope without first opening it.

Another way to arouse your prospects' curiosity is to make your envelope more personalized than the average direct mail piece. Use stamps instead of a postage meter. Put a sticker or seal on the envelope. For the ultimate personal touch, handwrite the address instead of using a printer or labels. Each of these tactics requires a little more time and effort, but if your prospect opens the envelope, it's worth it.

Yet another option is to print a message on the envelope that grabs your prospects' attention. The message can be serious or humorous, depending on how you want your company to be perceived. Consider messages like:

- Here's the information you requested.
- Information on the new tax law changes.
- Free (your area of specialty) report enclosed.
- Survey results enclosed.
- Free sample inside (naturally you only want to do this if you *have* in fact enclosed a free sample).
- Read me first—I'm not a bill!
- Open me quick! I can't breathe!
- For your eyes only.
- Letter opener tester.
- Things and stuff enclosed.

A couple of quick words of caution. Be certain that any message you print is not misleading. Too many businesses try to scare or trick customers into opening their envelopes. Always conduct your business with the highest possible degree of ethics. Also, in this age of heightened alert regarding terrorism, be sure that anything you print on an envelope (or enclose within) can't be mistaken for something dangerous. Postal workers and law enforcement officers tend to have (understandably) a poor sense of humor.

Once the envelope is opened, what will your prospects see? You only have a few seconds to hook their attention and entice them to read your entire letter, otherwise it will be crumpled up and tossed in the garbage can faster than you can say, "Have I got a deal for you."

The first thing to do is to use their name in the salutation of the letter. Pitches that begin, "Dear Homeowner" or "Dear Legal Professional," tend to get trashed. Letters that start out "Dear Ms. Johnson" or "Dear Frank" come across as more personal and buy you a few more seconds of attention. Any decent word processing program will allow you to do a mail merge—that is, merge the names from a database (your mailing list) into your letter.

Next, you need to grab them with a strong opening line. Your letter's first sentence is the equivalent of the headline in an advertisement. If the opening line intrigues your prospect, they'll read on. If it doesn't, they won't. So when crafting your first sentence, think headline. It needs to immediately address a need, a problem, a desire, or a concern.

The body of your letter should focus on benefits to the customer rather than features of your product or service, as we discussed earlier. List as many benefits as possible and be specific about them. You can make your case stronger by mentioning a guarantee and including testimonials from other customers.

Finally, close with a call to action. Direct them to contact you via one or more of the response options we listed above. Give your prospect a deadline to react, or else your letter may end up on their desk underneath a whole bunch of other offers.

P.S.: *Always include a P.S.* A P.S. is often the first thing people read in a letter and always the last thing they read. Use this opportunity to restate your guarantee, reiterate your special offer, or reaffirm the offer's deadline.

Postcards

In many ways, postcards are superior to letters. They're faster and easier to produce, they cost less to mail, and there's no envelope to open so they tend to get read right away. While a postcard gives you less writing space than a letter, it gives you the opportunity to communicate graphically, using drawings, logos, or photos. As a result, they can create much more impact on the recipient.

Here are some of the many ways to use postcards:

- Product or service introductions
- Announcements

- Reminders
- Invitations
- Coupons
- Contest entries
- Special offers
- Mini-newsletters

When a print shop creates your postcards, they don't print your design on a tiny piece of card stock. Instead, they lay out the same design six, eight, or ten times on a single printing plate and cut the resulting piece into individual cards. So, for example, if you want 800 postcards of a single design, the printer will print 100 sheets (with eight postcards per sheet) and cut them to make 800 cards.

So here's a money-saving tip: You can create several different postcards and have the printer lay them all out on the same sheet of paper. You could conceivably have your printer lay out eight different designs, print 800 sheets, and after the cards are cut, you'll have 800 each of eight different postcards. You'll save the setup charge on the other seven designs and your cost per piece will fall dramatically.

Newsletters

As home-based business owners, three of our biggest challenges are name recognition, credibility, and value perception. For this reason, a newsletter is a potent marketing weapon. A good newsletter keeps your name in front of your target audience, positions you as an expert, and provides added value to your clients and prospects. And publishing a newsletter from your home is relatively easy.

First, you need to know for whom you are writing. If people are going to spend their valuable time reading your newsletter, they must find the material of interest. So the first thing you have to decide is who your intended audience is. (Hint: "Everybody" is the wrong answer.) What goes into your newsletter, then, will depend on what that group's specific needs are.

Keep in mind that a newsletter is not an ad. People *don't* want to read pages of ad copy. They *do* want timely, interesting information that they can use to solve their problems. You want to give your readers ideas, facts, instructions, entertainment, statistics, resources, and/or inspiration. For instance, a small business marketing company Bev knows sends a quarterly newsletter to clients and prospective clients with marketing and publicity tips they can use in their business.

However, you don't have to write everything yourself. You can often recruit other people to write articles for you. Don teamed up with two other home-based business owners to produce a newsletter called "Money, Marketing and More," a bimonthly publication that actually generated subscription revenue.

Another option is to reprint (with permission) articles written by other experts in your field or a related field. Go to the Web site for the National Speakers Association (www.nsaspeaker.org) and search for people who speak on a topic that would be a good fit for your newsletter. Contact them and ask for permission to reprint an article you're interested in. They will often be happy to let you do so.

This is not to say that you can't do any actual marketing within your newsletter. You can (and should) include some promotional material, but as a general rule it should be about 25 percent or less of your text.

Once you have your content, you have to lay it out effectively. It's not enough just to have good, relevant information. It also has to look nice. Fortunately, there are a host of desktop publishing programs available that will help you create an attractive layout. Most also include clip art that you can use to add impact to your text. You can get additional ideas by looking at the newsletters you receive and noticing what you like and don't like about their appearance. Or you can hire a graphic designer to create a basic look for your newsletter, then for each issue you just have to fill in the blanks.

A consistent publishing schedule is important to the success of a newsletter as a marketing tool. You need to make sure it goes out to your target audience regularly. For this reason, you want to choose a publishing frequency that will allow you to consistently produce a quality publication in a timely manner. Popular schedules include monthly, bimonthly, and quarterly.

Once your newsletter is printed, send a copy to everyone who has ever done business with you and everyone you would like to do business with. Take them with you to trade shows and business functions. If possible, have copies placed in libraries, supermarkets, health clubs, small business development centers, or anyplace else your target audience might see them. Remember, the more prospects who see your newsletter, the more customers you'll get.

Coupon Books

You've probably received these little booklets at your home, filled with coupons for local restaurants, dry cleaners, hair salons, and specialty stores. They are mailed to every house in a particular zip code, so you can't pick and choose where your coupon ends up. But if the distribution matches your target area, it can be a cost-effective way to put your coupon into the hands of a lot of prospects.

Before you sign a contract, however, talk with some of the other business owners who advertise in the books to find out what their experience with the booklet company has been, what kind of results they've had, and any helpful lessons they've learned.

Postcard Decks

A postcard deck is literally a deck of postcards from different businesses bundled together and bulk mailed as one piece. Think of them as coupon books for businesses. Each postcard is a response tool with the offer on one side and the postage-paid return information on the other. An interested prospect needs only to fill out his or her contact information and drop the postcard in the mail.

It's fairly easy to set up an account with the post office for postage-paid return mail. This means you only pay for those replies that actually come back to you. Speak with the postmaster of your local branch office for more information.

Just as with coupon books, it's a good idea to talk with some of the other businesses that have used the deck you're considering. Not only can you discover if the particular deck is a good fit for your business, you may pick up some tips on how to make your postcard more effective.

PUBLICITY

Consistent use of publicity should be an integral part of your overall marketing strategy. It will allow you to reach large numbers of people for virtually no cost while at the same time giving you credibility you cannot buy in an advertisement.

Bear in mind that advertising is very different from publicity. In advertising, you are *paying* someone to mass distribute a *sales-oriented* message. Publicity is usually *free* and focuses on a *community-oriented* message. Through publicity, you are working to increase your name recognition and create awareness of your business, product, or service. Use the following strategies to kick your publicity machine into high gear and generate more sales.

Press Releases

The media needs you. An editor's job is to fill space. A radio or TV producer's job is to fill airtime. Both are looking for entertaining stories or useful information that will make people want to watch, listen to, or read what they produce. That's where you come in. You can create a press release about anything as long as it's of potential interest to that media outlet's audience. In other words: Is it a story?

Starting up your business? That's a story. Hired a new employee? That's a story. Tips on taking care of your lawn and garden? You guessed it, that's a story.

You can even generate multiple press releases for a single story. For example, you could set up a scholarship in the name of your business at your local high school or community college—even if it's only $50 or $100. Send a press release announcing the creation of the scholarship. Send another one announcing the event at which the scholarship will be awarded, and send a third announcing the recipient. A photo of you with a deserving student is positive publicity you can't buy.

Another way to leverage a press release is to offer something free. For instance, if you are a CPA and the IRS has just issued new rulings on tax laws affecting small businesses or personal tax returns, you might produce a tax tip booklet. Once it's developed, write a press release with a headline like "Free Booklet Explains Latest Tax Changes" and send it to your local newspapers, radio stations, and local TV news shows. Offer the booklet free with a self-addressed, stamped envelope (SASE), and offer yourself for interviews regarding the changes.

(A word of warning: Make sure you're prepared for an avalanche of requests for what you are offering. If you only anticipate 100 requests and you get 1,000 instead, the media will receive 900 complaints that the offer wasn't fulfilled, and you'll never be asked back! Create far more than you think you'll need. You can always give away the extras at other events.)

Here are some other press release ideas:

- Laid-off employee competes with former employer.
- Family who never saw one another now spends all day together.
- Local community has surprisingly high number of home-based businesses.

- Business celebrates first, fifth, tenth, etc. anniversary.
- Local business wins major contract.
- Tips for other home businesses.
- Stay-at-home parent raises kids and profits.
- Local business mentors tomorrow's business leaders.

One way to make your press release relevant and timely on a consistent basis is to link it to recurring seasonal events. Besides the big traditional holidays (Thanksgiving, Christmas, Valentine's Day, Fourth of July, etc.), think about other holiday occasions both religious (Passover, Ramadan, Ash Wednesday) and secular (Arbor Day, Chinese New Year, Secretary's Week). You can find information on these and other annual occasions at your library in books such as *Chase's Calendar of Events*. Also consider such recurring themes as back-to-school, tax season, and summer vacation. And don't forget Small Business Week in May and Home-Based Business Week in October!

Keep in mind that journalists are flooded by dozens or even hundreds of press releases daily. Since they don't have time to read and evaluate each one carefully, they scan quickly and make snap judgments. To maximize the chances of your press release being read and used, follow these media friendly guidelines:

- Be brief (one page is preferred) but get the most important or intriguing facts in. If reporters need more information, they'll contact you.
- Write a good headline. Read your local newspaper to learn the style of headline writing they use and try to write your headline in the same style.
- Include the who, what, where, and when in the first paragraph. This may be all that gets printed.
- Use simple, declarative sentences.
- Write in the third person. Act as if you are the writer or interviewer, using *he* or *she* instead of *I, me,* or *mine.*
- Print your press release on your business stationery, double-spaced with one-inch margins all around.
- Learn whether each specific newspaper, radio station, or other outlet prefers to have information sent to them via postal mail, fax, or e-mail.

Each time you send out a press release, keep a copy of it, as well as the list of contacts to which you sent it. Be sure to include your press releases—even if they were never published—in your marketing kit. The fact that you've sent out press releases automatically gives you credibility.

And keep the PR generator running! Don't plan one publicity campaign and expect to ride that wave forever. You may not even get noticed the first time. Perseverance is the key to getting publicity. Make a publicity calendar and plan something every quarter, or more often if you can manage it.

Articles

Virtually every trade association and business group has a newsletter, magazine, or journal. And they are all in need of articles of value to their members. Such articles must be informational, not promotional in nature. They should be of general interest or targeted to the specific needs of the readers.

Start with the organizations to which you belong. Contact the editors of their publications and ask about needs, schedules, and editorial guidelines. Write according to their guidelines and include your contact information for the authorship credit. If they will also print your picture, that's ideal, but even just getting your name and company name in print will give you valuable exposure and credibility. Once your article is published, be sure to get reprints to include in your promotional materials.

Awards

Many business organizations give out annual awards in a variety of categories. Nominate yourself for any and every award for which you are eligible, then send out a press release announcing the nomination. If you become a finalist or a winner, send out additional press releases. With this strategy, you can get multiple exposures from a single effort, not even counting the publicity you may get from the sponsoring organization. You also receive the side benefit of being portrayed in an inherently positive light.

Naturally, any time you win an award, you want to include that information in your marketing materials. When Completed Systems—a Fairfax, Virginia, technology company that began as a home-based business—was named "IT Business of the Year" by their local Chamber of Commerce, they created stickers to tout the accolade. The stickers were attached to all their marketing materials, instantly updating them and giving the company greater credibility. Another example: A basket maker in Albany, New York, placed a basket in the county fair and won a blue ribbon. All his marketing materials now include the phrase "blue ribbon baskets."

Opinion Pieces

Write op-ed (short for "opposite editorial") pieces or send letters to the editor on issues that relate to home-based business, your industry, or your community. Consider issues such as taxes, child care, transportation, and government regulation.

Appearing in the editorial section automatically increases your credibility and positions you as someone who cares about your community, not just making money. Use a combination of facts (with sources) and emotional stories to best make your case. Don't try to actively promote your business, just stick to the issue at hand.

Although you have a greater chance of getting published in smaller magazines and newspapers because there's less competition for op-ed space, you'll get greater exposure and credibility in larger publications, so direct your efforts at both types.

FACE-TO-FACE MARKETING

If you're like many home-based businesses, your prospects can't come to you. Fortunately, *you* can go to *them*. Marketing to your prospects in person can be time-consuming, but can also be highly effective. When your prospects meet you in person, you have an opportunity to establish a relationship with them. It even gives you an advantage over your larger competitors because people typically prefer to do business with someone they know, rather than a large, faceless entity.

Networking
Networking is without question the single most potent marketing tool that a home business owner has. It is low cost and has a high return, with a great deal of flexibility. But like any tool, it is most effective when used properly. Recognizing some fundamental truths about networking will help you be more successful at it.

First of all, let's be clear about what networking is and is not. Networking is not selling. Networking and selling are both components of marketing (and every salesperson should be a good networker), but they are very different things. Selling involves persuading, informing, and negotiating. Networking is about meeting people and getting to know them. Once people know you, they're more likely to buy from you.

This does not mean that if you dash into a room, hand out 40 business cards, and race home to wait for the phone to ring that you're a good networker. On the contrary, networking, like other forms of marketing, requires commitment, repetition, and a long-term focus. Consequently, our definition of networking is: meeting people and building long-term relationships with them.

Here are some quick tips for networking:

1. Wear your name badge on the right side. When you shake hands with someone, their line of sight will naturally go to your name tag, since everyone shakes hands with their right hand (even lefties).
2. Wear clothes with two pockets. Keep your business cards in one pocket and the business cards you receive in the other pocket. Carry a pen or pencil in one of your pockets so you can make any notes needed on the business card you receive. It will be easier to remember why you have that card when you get back to the office.
3. Carry several business cards with you no matter where you go, including personal activities. Bev and Don have given out business cards (when appropriate) at wedding receptions, baseball games, church picnics, and while on vacation in other parts of the country.

One of the keys to getting to know people is asking questions. Ask about the other person's business, kids, golf game, whatever is appropriate for the circumstances. Asking questions demonstrates that you're interested in the other person and gives you an opportunity to learn potentially valuable information. And it's a fact of human nature that if you give people a chance to talk about themselves, they'll think you're a great conversationalist!

After you've met somebody, it's critical to follow up. Remember, people will usually need to feel like they know you and trust you before they buy from you. This requires time and repeated contact. Send letters, make phone calls, and give referrals whenever possible. If you have a newsletter, put them on your mailing list. And don't ignore someone just because you don't think they're a good sales prospect. You never know who might become a referral source, an information provider, or a lead to another valuable contact. Treat every person you meet with respect, warmth, and kindness. Your goal should be to build friendships first—everything else will follow naturally.

Leads Groups

These groups, which go by various names—referral groups, tip clubs, resource groups—exist for the sole purpose of networking. They may be nonprofit or for-profit. Members are expected to generate leads for other members on a regular basis. For that reason, membership is limited to one company per industry— for example, one lawyer, one printer, one florist, one insurance agent, etc. Meetings are typically weekly or biweekly over breakfast. Be aware, these groups are serious and require a real commitment on your part. Members can be expelled for missing too many meetings or not providing enough referrals.

Trade Shows

A lot of home-based businesses don't include trade shows as part of their marketing mix because of the relatively high investment involved. But while a trade show may be more expensive than most other marketing tools, it can also produce greater and faster results.

The costliest, most time-consuming part of marketing is trying to locate and reach your specific target market. Now imagine if everyone in your target market showed up at the same place at the same time for you to talk with. That's the value of a trade show.

A trade show is also a great equalizer. At most shows, your booth space will be exactly the same as the vast majority of exhibitors. This instantly gives you the same kind of credibility that everyone else at the show has.

A trade show does require a lot of preparation and effort to maximize the value of your investment. You have to consider what your exhibit is going to look like, how you're going to attract people to you, what you'll say to prospects, and how you're going to follow up with them after the show. The more you plan and prepare, the better your results will be.

The best shows for you are those targeted at a specific market: bridal shows, home and garden expos, sporting goods shows, and so on. If your target audience is a particular profession or kind of business, check out the trade associations that serve them. Associations often produce a trade show in conjunction with their annual conference, giving you access to hundreds or thousands of decision makers.

If you manufacture a product that you want to get into retail stores, think about the kinds of stores where your product would fit best, and exhibit at the shows their owners or buyers attend to find new products. Hat Flags, for example, a Germantown, Maryland, home-based creator of pennants that can be attached to caps and visors, exhibits at shows geared toward college bookstores and shows aimed at distributors of advertising specialties.

Volunteering

Volunteering enables you to help your business while you help your community. It raises your profile, gives you opportunities to hone important skills, and positions you as a caring individual. People learn about you and are motivated to do business with you not because of your marketing message, but because people prefer to buy from people they like and feel good about. Volunteering should always be part of your business activities, not just because it's good marketing, but because it's the right thing to do.

Cooper's maxim: Good things happen to people who do good things.

Speeches and Seminars

There are hundreds of local groups that need experts to speak to their members at weekly or monthly meetings. Such groups range from business organizations (Chambers of Commerce and trade associations) to service clubs (Rotary, Lions, Kiwanis, Optimist, Moose, Knights of Columbus, etc.).

As with written articles, these business speeches need to be informational rather than promotional in nature. Most presentations of this type run between 10 and 30 minutes. Check what the time limit will be in advance and plan to shorten your presentation if the meeting runs long. Provide handouts so that everybody walks out of the room with your contact information.

If your public speaking skills are not as good as you would like them to be, join a Toastmasters Club or work with a speech coach to hone your skills. A side benefit of speaking to groups is that you'll become better at making sales presentations as well.

TELEPHONE MARKETING

The telephone is the most common and most basic marketing tool at our disposal, yet it's all too often ignored. On the phone, you sound just as professional as any other business, so it's a tool you should make good use of.

Cold Calling

The idea of making cold calls can strike fear into the hearts of even the most seasoned salespeople. But cold calling is fast, free, and, if done correctly, effective. It's one of the absolute best options for a new home-business owner with little or no marketing budget who needs to make sales immediately. There are hundreds of sales books that will teach you how to succeed at cold calling. Check out the resources section under the heading "Sales" for some of the best.

Voice Mail Message

When prospects call you and you're not there, what do they hear? If it's the standard, "Hi, I'm unavailable, please leave a message" spiel, you're missing out on a great marketing opportunity. Use your outgoing message to give your caller more information and options. Consider including in your message:

- What you do
- Your schedule for the day or week
- Your cell phone number
- Your e-mail address
- The address for your Web site and a reason to visit it
- A current special or something else to ask you about

In Bev's Hat Flags business, the voice mail message gives the company name and then the slogan: "Visible Symbols of Loyalty." The message is updated with additional information when they are scheduled to exhibit their product. Keep your message as brief as possible in order to hold the caller's attention while he or she is waiting for the beep to leave a message.

Message on Hold

Odds are you're going to be using a very simple one- or two-line phone, at least at first. But if you graduate to a more sophisticated multiline phone system, consider purchasing a message-on-hold system. That way, when your clients or prospects are on hold, they can listen to something other than silence. Your on-hold message might include recent or past achievements, current or upcoming specials, helpful tips, or even testimonials from happy customers.

ONLINE MARKETING

On the Internet, nobody knows your business is home-based. Unless, of course, you want them to know. The Web is the great equalizer. With a little knowledge, a little effort, and a little money, you can create an online presence that outmarkets and outsells businesses far bigger than yours.

Web Site

There are five primary characteristics of an effective Web site:

1. It has lots of information that visitors perceive as valuable.
2. It is updated frequently.
3. It downloads quickly.
4. It is easy to navigate.
5. It is promoted well.

Notice that "It has lots of flashy graphics and animation" is not on the list. An effective Web site is much more about substance than style. As a general rule, the more content, the more people will like it. And the more frequently it's updated, the more frequently visitors will return.

So what kinds of content can you put on your Web site to attract people to it? Here are some ideas:

- Articles
- Tips
- Quizzes and self-tests
- Trivia
- Quotations
- Industry news
- A contest
- Templates
- Guidelines
- Fact sheets
- FAQs (Frequently Asked Questions)
- A blog (a Web log or diary)
- Thought for the day
- Resource list
- Photos
- Diagrams
- Recipes
- Step-by-step instructions
- Reviews
- Gift ideas
- Message boards
- Customer success stories
- A guest book
- Surveys

But no matter how much great content is on your site, no one will find it unless you promote the site itself. "If you build it, they will come" does not apply to the Web. Because of the sheer volume of sites out there, you have to actively market your site to get people to visit.

According to Jupiter Communications, a company that tracks Web usage, the number one way people find Web sites is through printed materials. So make sure you put your Web address on *everything*—your business cards, brochures, advertising specialties, yellow pages ad, and anything else your name is printed on.

The second most common way people find Web sites is via links from other sites. So look for opportunities to create mutual links with sites that complement yours.

The third most common way that people find Web sites is through search engines. Your Web designer or Web host should be able to submit your site to the major search engines for you. Be aware that each search engine uses different criteria to rank Web sites, and those criteria change frequently. For that reason, your site needs to be re-sent to the major search engines periodically.

E-mail

E-mail is one of the best marketing tools ever invented. You can send a message to one person or millions at basically no cost. Unfortunately, this ease and lack of expense have led to the scourge of "spam"—unsolicited marketing e-mails by the millions that clutter in-boxes and crash servers. In the early days of the Web, when the average person only received two or three unsolicited messages a day, direct marketing by e-mail was viewed as simply akin to postal direct mail. But with its uncontrolled growth, spam has gone from mildly annoying to absolutely maddening. If you send out an unsolicited marketing e-mail, you're likely to generate more animosity than sales, so your best bet is to avoid it altogether.

This is not to say that you can't use e-mail to market your business. You just have to use it in the right way. E-mail is a perfect tool to stay in touch with customers and prospects that have given you the "okay" to market to them. People you meet at networking functions, who visit your Web site, and who request information from you can be safely e-mailed. The keys are to:

- Request their e-mail address.
- Send them information they'll find useful.
- Respect their privacy by not sharing their information with anyone.
- Don't flood them with messages.
- Give them an opportunity to decline future messages from you.

Be sure to create an e-mail signature. A signature is composed of several lines of text that you create once, and then it's automatically added to the end of every e-mail you send out. It can contain your name, business name, contact information, slogan, and anything else you want to include. One thing you want to be sure your signature contains is a hyperlink to your Web site along with a reason for clicking on it. Your e-mail program should have an option under "Tools" for creating an e-mail signature.

E-zine

If a paper newsletter is too complicated, time-consuming, or expensive for you, consider publishing an electronic alternative. An e-zine—as electronic newsletters are called—doesn't have the tactile feel of a paper newsletter, but its other advantages make up for it.

- It doesn't need graphics and layout.
- You can create one in a matter of minutes.

- It costs you nothing to send it.
- You can make it as short or as long as you want it to be.

Because an e-zine costs you basically nothing to send out, you can publish it as frequently as you want.

Online Auctions

Yahoo! Auctions, eBay, and other online auctions can be a great way of selling your products all over the world at low cost and with little or no risk. Many people have built entire home-based businesses just by creating "stores" on eBay, where they sell or resell all kinds of merchandise.

Chat Rooms and Discussion Groups

There are hundreds of thousands of chat rooms and discussion groups throughout the Internet on every conceivable topic under the sun. Locate and visit some of the ones that relate to your business or area of expertise. After you've read enough of the discussion to feel comfortable, feel free to join in the virtual conversation.

DO NOT, however, use these forums to purely plug your business. In most chat rooms and discussion groups, blatant advertising is forbidden, and even if it isn't, you'll generate a lot of resentment on the part of the other participants.

Instead, think of these virtual conversations as the online equivalent of networking. Focus first on the topic that people are gathered to discuss. Give people a chance to get to know you, and *then* you can mention what you do.

GIVEAWAY MARKETING

The most powerful four-letter word in marketing is "free." Everybody loves getting something for nothing. Giving things away creates goodwill, puts your name and even your products in the hands of prospects, and demonstrates that you're a trustworthy company your customer can have confidence in.

Advertising Specialties

An advertising specialty (or promotional product) is any item with your name on it that is intended to be given away to prospects and customers for promotional purposes. A good ad specialty keeps your name in front of your prospects on a regular basis.

The best ad specialties are durable items that your target market perceives as both useful and valuable. The more useful, the more it will stay in front of your prospects; and the more valuable, the more your prospects will appreciate it. And you.

There is an astounding variety of advertising specialties in every price range. Here are some items you may want to consider:

- Coffee mugs
- Plastic cups
- Water bottles
- Insulated foam beverage holders
- Letter openers
- T-shirts
- Pens
- Notepads
- Hats
- Swiss army knives
- Tool kits

As you choose which ad specialties you want to use for your business, keep in mind that whatever you give away will reflect on your business. Since, as a home-based business, it's especially important to project a professional image, you'll want to select items that reflect the quality of your company.

An advertising specialties professional can help you determine the best options for your business, prospects, and budget. You can find a person who specializes in promotional products through your local Chamber of Commerce, in the yellow pages, or via the Web. They may even be another home-based business!

Calendars

According to the American Calendar Marketing Association, the average person looks at a calendar five times a day. Which means a calendar can be a great way to keep your name in front of a prospect for an entire year. Consider customizing your calendar with your picture or with pictures of your products, services, or even customers.

Magnets

If you want your prospects to see your phone number every day, their refrigerator door is a hard location to beat. You can have magnets custom made in your logo, a silhouette, or in any of a variety of shapes and colors for a reasonable cost. Or you can go to an office supply store and buy magnets that you can attach your business card to, turning your card (or any other similar-sized piece of paper) into a magnet.

Bookmarks

Anyone can create bookmarks with a minimum of skill, equipment, and cost. All you need is a computer, a printer, and a paper cutter. Any design or desktop publishing software will do, and if you don't have that, you can even use a word processing program.

Make them as plain or as fancy as you want, just be sure you have your full contact information on them, especially your Web site. You might want to include some tips, a couple of testimonials, or a listing of your products and services. (Remember, you have two sides to work with!)

You can print your bookmarks in color or in black on colored card stock. If you don't own a paper cutter, you can take your bookmarks to a local print shop to have them cut. If you have a laminating machine, laminating your bookmarks will make them look better and last longer, but it's not absolutely necessary.

Free Samples or Consultations

Any unknown product or service has to overcome a prospect's indifference in order to succeed. Consumers and business buyers both already have preferences regarding what they buy and are wary about spending money on something new and unproven. Simply put, most people are happy with what they're already buying, and trying a new product or vendor isn't worth the risk of disappointment.

Free trials eliminate that risk. (Heck, if it's free, why *not* try it?) So if your offering is superior, or unique, or something you have to experience to truly appreciate, one of the best things you can do is give it away.

If you sell a product, give away a full-size or trial-size sample. If you sell a service, offer a free first session. For example, a massage therapist might offer a free 15-minute massage, while an attorney or a consultant might offer a free one-hour consultation. A great first experience is likely to turn into a sale.

Like many experts who speak professionally, we both charge thousands of dollars per speech. But we speak free of charge for many community and service organizations, as well as certain nonprofit groups and conferences. Partly it's a way for us to give back to our communities. At the same time, it's excellent marketing for us because often somebody in one of those audiences will want to hire us to speak to *their* organization.

Information

One of the best things you can give away is information, because it has a high perceived value, but it typically costs you nothing. You can offer articles or white papers you've written, reports you've compiled, or surveys you've conducted. These don't have to be elaborate or scientific, as long as they will be valuable to your target audience.

For example, you might offer an article on:

- What you need to know before you retire.
- Ten tips for organizing your office space.
- Trends in medical billing.
- How to choose an interior designer.
- Staying healthy during cold and flu season.
- Recent changes in labor laws.

We both have articles on a variety of subjects on our Web sites that you can read free of charge with no strings attached. Just go to www.Beverley Williams.com and www.DonCooper.com.

Donations for Community Groups

Don't just limit your generosity to direct prospects. There are dozens or hundreds of local nonprofit groups in your community that could greatly benefit while giving you an excellent publicity opportunity. Consider donating your products or services (or gift certificates) to local service clubs or charitable organizations for their use, to give away as prizes or to auction off to raise money. The organization gets something of value while you get a trial usage, a tax deduction, and free publicity.

ELECTRONIC MARKETING

Electronic marketing tools require a bigger investment than many other tools, but they can be extremely powerful. An electronic marketing piece can position you as highly professional and technologically advanced. To do it right (which is the only way to do it), you'll need help from audiovisual professionals, unless, of course, that's your business. Talk to one about your goals, your market, and your budget before you undertake a project like this.

Audiotapes or CDs

People can't read your brochure while they drive. (Well, they *can*, but they shouldn't.) But they can easily listen to an audio brochure on a tape or CD. Putting your marketing message on audiotape or CD is as easy as writing a script, practicing it, and sitting down in a studio to record it. An audio brochure gives you the opportunity to convey emotional factors to your prospects via your voice: confidence, enthusiasm, concern, and more.

Since an audio recording has no visual component, you'll need to keep your prospect's attention by varying your rate, tone, and volume. Add variety by having some of your customers provide testimonials in their own words and voices. Or consider using a question-and-answer format, with a friend interviewing you as the expert.

Be sure to make your recording on some kind of digital media. That way, if you have a CD burner, you can make as many CDs as you need right in your home.

CD-ROMs

Imagine if your brochure had audio and video clips. And a PowerPoint presentation. And about 20 times the number of pages. That's what you can do with a CD-ROM. It's much more expensive than a paper brochure, but it can make a much bigger impact, especially if your business relates to technology.

You have two basic choices for the format of your disc: full-size or mini-CDs. Full-size discs are the standard ones you see everywhere. While they're familiar and inexpensive, they are also cumbersome in large quantities and unexciting to look at. Mini-CDs use the same technology as their larger siblings but are cut smaller, so they're more convenient to carry around. You can get discs that are the size and approximate shape of a business card or that are cut in a wide variety of shapes. The downsides are that they hold less data than a full-size disc and they only work in computers with CD-ROM drives that have a sliding tray.

The easiest way to create a CD-ROM brochure is to simply put your Web site on a CD. But if you're going to make use of this technology, be as creative as you can and incorporate as many of the advantages of the technology as possible. And be sure your CD brochure is compatible with both Windows and Macintosh computers.

ADVERTISING

The American Marketing Association defines advertising as "mass paid communication, the purpose of which is to impart information, develop attitudes, and induce favorable action for the advertiser." There are three key elements to this definition.

The first is the word "mass." One of the unique advantages of advertising is that it reaches many people at once. As a result, it can be tremendously efficient, giving you access to hundreds, thousands, even millions of people.

The second key characteristic is the word "paid." If it's free, it's not advertising. Costs vary based on the size and type of the audience reached, the length or size of the ad, the demand for advertising in general, and other factors. The price can be anywhere from $20 for a three-line classified ad in a local newspaper to more than $1 million for a spot during the Super Bowl.

The third key element consists of the three above-mentioned purposes: "to impart information, develop attitudes, and induce favorable action for the advertiser." You have to do all three to sell your product or service. Your prospect needs information about you, your company, and your offering. Next, you have to foster positive attitudes about who you are and what you sell, thereby stimulating interest, desire, and trust among your prospects. Finally, you must persuade your prospects to take some action, which can mean sending for more information, visiting your Web site, or calling you to buy. Advertising of any sort can do at least one of those tasks. Truly *effective* advertising does all three things simultaneously.

Given the wide variety of free and low-cost marketing tools we've discussed here, you might wonder why you'd want to buy advertising, which is typically more expensive than the other options. The answer is that advertising gives you a tremendous amount of control over the message and enables you to convey that message to a potentially huge audience.

As a home-based business, it also gives you credibility. Your prospects judge you in part by the environment in which they see you. Psychologically, when people see your ad, they assign roughly the same degree of professionalism to you that they do to everyone else whose ad appears with yours.

One other thing to keep in mind about advertising: The rates sales reps quote you aren't cast in stone. They are usually negotiable. Sometimes *extremely* negotiable. So ask for a great deal on any of the following advertising vehicles. You just might get it.

Yellow Pages Ads

Even with the Internet, many people still turn to their local yellow pages when they're ready to buy something and are looking for a source. Whether the yellow pages is a good vehicle for you depends on whether people look there for *your* type of business. For example, people don't look for professional speakers in the yellow pages, so you won't find either Bev or Don there. But people *do* look for delivery services there, so the courier service that Don and his father operated had a prominent display ad.

If the yellow pages is an important place for your business to be, you want to maximize the value of your presence.

- Purchase the largest ad you can afford. Larger ads draw more response.
- Use color to stand out on the page.
- Have your graphic designer create your ad for you.
- Fill all the space in your ad with as much relevant information as possible. "White space" is pointless in this medium.
- If you accept credit cards, mention that fact.
- Make sure your words are easily readable, even by people with poor eyesight.
- Include all your contact information, *especially* your Web address.
- If your business fits under more than one business category, buy a display ad in the category people are most likely to look in first, and buy small ads under the other categories, stating: "See our ad under _____."

Newspaper Display Ads

The most critical element of a newspaper display ad is the headline. With all the competition on the page for the reader's eye, your headline must reach out and grab your prospect's attention. Browse through your local paper and compare the headlines of the ads on each page. Notice the similarities and differences and what attracts your attention at first glance.

The next most important element is the offer. Give your prospect a reason to respond to your ad immediately. Be sure to include your contact information and Web address.

Like a yellow pages ad, graphic design plays a role in your newspaper ad's effectiveness. Tell your graphic designer what you want in your ad and let them create it for you. Ideally, you can use a newspaper display ad as a flyer and vice versa, getting two marketing pieces for the price of one.

One final element in the success of a newspaper display ad is its consistency. A one-shot ad is virtually worthless. Your ad needs to run a couple dozen times or more before you can realistically expect to see results. When it comes to your budget, if you have to choose between size and frequency, go with frequency.

Classified Ads

If you can't afford display ads (or even if you can), consider classified ads as a less expensive alternative. Businesses of all sizes use the classifieds to reach thousands of readers. Because the ads in a classified section are grouped by subject matter, it's easy for people who are looking for your type of product or service to find you.

Classified ads give you a lot of flexibility, which means you can experiment at little cost. Test different headlines, copy lengths, offers, even different wording to discover what works best. You can also play with boldface type, uppercase type, and, in some newspapers, graphic symbols. When you find a formula that delivers great results, keep your ad in there consistently.

Magazine Ads

Magazine advertisements are typically more expensive than newspaper ads, but they give you more credibility. Magazines also give you better opportunities to target your message to a specific audience. Research which magazines your ideal prospects read and compare them for circulation numbers, demographic breakdowns, and price. That will enable you to choose the best magazine for your goals.

Keep in mind that when you purchase an ad in a magazine, you don't necessarily have to pay for the whole country to see it. Many magazines publish regional editions, and advertising in just your local region can make this an affordable option for you.

Ads in Newsletters

As a general rule, the more targeted your ad, the better your response will be. And because newsletters are typically targeted at a specific type of reader, they can be excellent vehicles for your ads. For example, if your target market is attorneys, there are numerous legal newsletters you can advertise in.

A newsletter ad is much like a magazine or newspaper display ad, so follow the same guidelines for creating an effective advertisement. If a newsletter you'd like to be in doesn't accept advertising, see if you can get an article published in it.

Ads in Programs

Every event needs a program. And every program needs ads. And those ads frequently get read by audience members waiting for the event to start. If the attendees of a particular event fit your target customer profile, consider placing an ad in it. Buying ads in the programs for a *series* of events will get you a greater return than a program for a single event because of the repetition of your message.

Ads in Directories

If you belong to an organization, you're listed in its directory. And if the other members of the organization use that directory, you can raise your profile in it by placing an ad. The advantage of a directory is that unlike a program or a magazine, a directory is likely to be kept around for a year or even longer.

CUSTOMER MARKETING

Your absolute, most important audience to market to is your existing customers. Studies have shown that, on average, it costs five times as much to gain a new customer as it does to sell to an existing customer. To get new customers, you have to expose them to several marketing messages because you have to break through the marketing clutter, catch their attention, inform them of who you are, build confidence in your company, persuade them you're the best option for them, and move them to action.

By contrast, with a person who's already your customer, all that hard work has already been done. Once they've bought from you—assuming their experience with you was a positive one—it takes a lot less time and effort on your part to sell to them again because they already know, like, and trust you.

This leads us to two conclusions. First, don't take your customers for granted, as too many companies do. Instead, treat them like gold, because they are your greatest potential source of revenue. And second, market consistently to your customers, because it will typically pay you far better dividends than any other marketing.

Obviously, you can use nearly all of the previous marketing tactics with your existing customer base. But here are some additional tools you can use specifically with your customers.

Customer Follow-Up

Think of your first transaction with a new customer not as closing a sale, but as opening a relationship. Call your customers periodically to see how they like your product or service. Determine when they're likely to need you again. Find out what other needs they have. Or just say hello.

Send direct mail letters and postcards aimed specifically at them. Offer customer-only specials or "customer appreciation deals." Send birthday or anniversary cards. Clip and send articles you think would be of interest to them.

The key is stay in touch with your customers so two things happen. First, you stay in their consciousness. Out of sight, out of mind. You want to be sure they think of you when they're ready to buy again. Second, your customer feels that you appreciate and care about him or her—not just as a revenue source, but as a person. That's something the average person can't get from most companies, and it's one of your biggest competitive advantages. When your customers feel that you care about them, you're the one they want to spend their money with.

Invoices

An invoice is more than just a tool to collect on services already rendered. It's also a prime marketing opportunity. You already have to spend the postage, so why not make the envelope do double duty? Include a brochure, a flyer, or a coupon for a future purchase.

Frequent Buyer Program

If you want your customers to come back to you again and again, give them an incentive. A frequent buyer program rewards their loyalty and their frequency with a free item or service after a certain number are purchased. You probably have one or more from various businesses in your wallet or purse right now.

You can make frequent buyer cards yourself in your home. Like bookmarks, just lay them out with any desktop publishing or word processing software, print them on colored card stock, and cut them with a paper cutter. Use a custom stamp or hole puncher (available at office supply or arts and crafts stores) to keep track of your customer's purchases, and prepare to be amazed at how often your customers return to you.

Referrals

A person who is referred to you is five times as likely to buy from you as any other type of prospect. Instead of having to build trust with your prospect from the ground up, you have a head start because your prospect has trust in the friend that referred them.

Yet, too many home-business owners fail to ever ask for referrals. They don't want to appear greedy, they're concerned about bothering their customer, or they're simply afraid of rejection. But the truth is that your client *wants* to refer you. If you discover a great product or you get terrific service from some-place, you want your friends and family to know about it too, don't you?

So be sure to ask your customers for the names of people who might also benefit from your product or service. The best time to ask is after you have delivered value to them, when they're excited or appreciative. Here are some other helpful dos and don'ts:

Do

Ask every single customer

Ask periodically

Be specific, e.g. "who else in your family" or "who else in your country club"

Frame your request as a desire to help others the way you've help your client

Ask for a testimonial letter if they can't give you a name right now

Don't

Apologize for asking

Pressure your customers

Ask *too* often

Get upset if they can't think of a name

Whenever you do get a referral, it's critical to show your appreciation to the person who provided it. A basic psychological principle is that any behavior that is rewarded tends to be repeated, while behavior that's ignored tends to cease. If you give us a referral and we demonstrate our appreciation with a heartfelt thank you and perhaps a gift, you're likely to give us more. On the other hand, if you give us a referral and we don't acknowledge it, you almost certainly will never give us another.

At the very least, you should send a *handwritten* thank you note to your customer. Ideally, send a gift of some sort. The more significant the reward, the more likely it is that you'll get more referrals from your customer. It's also a good idea to send a thank you when you receive the referral and to send *another* thank you when the referred prospect buys.

COOPERATIVE MARKETING

So far we've discussed dozens of marketing strategies and tactics that are particularly well-suited for home-based businesses. There is one more strategy, however, that belongs in a category by itself: cooperative marketing. What we mean by this is working with another company, home-based or otherwise, to market each other or to market yourselves jointly.

Keep an eye out for other businesses that don't compete with you but serve the same market you do. For example, an attorney and an accountant. A realtor and a relocation company. A party planner and a caterer. Ask yourself: "What other needs do my clients have?" Businesses that serve those needs would then be potential marketing partners. You can pool your resources, market to each other's customers, and refer each other.

When you and another quality company team up to market together, everybody wins. You both get more bang from your marketing buck, and you get more opportunities without spending more money. And when you refer a customer to a business you partner with, your client gets their needs satisfied, your marketing partner get a new customer, and you get the appreciation of both of them. And the principle works the other way as well, when your partner sends you business.

So look for other companies with whom you can cooperate. Talk to them to determine their fit and willingness. And if you both decide to pursue joint marketing opportunities, here are some tactics you can consider:

- Purchase joint ads.
- Include each other's flyers or brochures in your invoices.
- Send your partner's coupons and frequent buyer cards to your customers.
- Share a trade show exhibit.
- Hand out each other's ad specialties and other giveaways.
- Volunteer together.
- Create links between your Web sites.
- Feature each other in your newsletters or e-zines.
- Join a leads group together or create your own.
- Mention or quote each other in articles and press releases.
- Hand out each other's business cards.

Just because you work alone doesn't mean you have to work *alone*. Partnering with another company to market cooperatively is a great way to leverage your marketing resources.

Chapter 11

WHAT HAPPENED TO THE WATER COOLER?

Dealing with the Isolation of Being Home Alone

What is isolation? *Webster's* dictionary defines *isolation* as "the condition of being isolated." And defines *isolate* as "to separate from a group or whole and set apart." The thesaurus lists other words for isolate: aloneness, loneliness, solitude, separated, and detached. So what?

Think about your work life up to now. If you work (or worked) for corporate America, you may share an office or work in a larger space shared by many. Maybe you're lucky enough to have your own office. Regardless, there are other people you interact with every workday. Your morning may start at the communal coffeepot or with a group meeting. You may even start your workday by going to your office before others normally arrive in order to have some quiet time to work on a project. Regardless of your scenario, you interact with others all through your workday. You probably don't think about this interaction unless it's to bemoan your lack of uninterrupted time to work.

Now imagine yourself in your own home office. Oh, the peace and quiet. No interruptions from coworkers. No stopping in the middle of work because someone wants to share what they did over the weekend. You are blissfully alone! The first few days or weeks will be splendid. You are energized and focused. For a few, this feeling will last longer, perhaps forever. For the rest, isolation can begin to set in once the initial time period has passed.

A survey by the American Association of Home-Based Businesses several years ago found that one of the things home-based entrepreneurs miss most from a corporate environment is interaction with coworkers.

Because most of us are in our houses all day, every day, we do not get as much opportunity to see and talk with people as those in typical offices do. It's easy to feel isolated when the only coworker you have is a clock ticking away. And while pets make terrific companions, they are not particularly good at answering questions or giving you feedback on your ideas.

What are the signs of isolation? It may come in the form of lack of productivity. You have things to do but you lack the energy or incentive to do them. You may find yourself spending hours over breakfast reading the newspaper. What to do?

This is where self-discipline comes in. You are the boss. You have to look over your own shoulder and give yourself a nudge to get going. A student in one of Bev's classes several years ago shared with the class his method for getting into a routine each workday morning. When he worked for corporate America, he normally went out the side door of his house to get into his car. It had been his habit to stop at a fast food restaurant to pick up a cup of coffee on his way to the office. Now that he was a home-based business owner, he decided to follow this routine. He left his home through the side door, got in his car, drove to the nearest fast food restaurant, bought a cup of coffee, and returned home. He then entered his office and was now at work.

Okay, this gets you into the office and perhaps in the frame of mind to focus on work, but it doesn't change the fact that you're alone. There is no one else to say good morning to or brainstorm a problem with. You need interaction with others. It's time to form a support network for yourself to avoid the isolation of being a home-based business owner.

Excessive isolation can lead to frustration, anger, and even depression. To prevent feelings of isolation, we have some strategies to suggest for reconnecting with people.

REACH OUT AND TOUCH SOMEONE

If your phone isn't ringing, make someone else's ring. Call friends and colleagues to share ideas, leads, challenges, and successes. Fax or e-mail them documents to get their feedback. Wish them happy birthday, happy anniversary, or happy anything else that's going on in their personal or professional lives. Using a contact manager makes this easy to do and to keep track of.

Call prospects, obviously. But call clients as well. Check up on your own work. Are your customers completely satisfied or could something be improved? Will they have new projects coming up soon? Do they have any other needs that you might be able to fill? An additional benefit of calling your customers is a stronger relationship with them. Such outstanding customer service can blow away your competition and keep you first in your clients' minds when they need your product or service again. This is one of the things home-based business owners have shown over the years: good customer service. And, as you've probably experienced yourself, good customer service is far too rare these days.

GET ONLINE

E-mail and instant messages (IMs) in some ways are even better than the telephone. They can be written and read at your convenience, yet still be timely. It is also a lot cheaper to e-mail or IM people across the country or around the world. It's easier to stay in touch with people who are either hard to reach by telephone or need to keep their phone free for clients to call.

Another way to use your modem to fight isolation is to log in to chat rooms or discussion groups. There are online forums for any topic you can think of, and they are great ways to make new friends and colleagues. Some interest groups you may want to explore include those for your local geographic area, your particular industry, or home-based businesses in general.

There are also online learning classes. If you've been meaning to take some courses but find it hard to get away from the home office, consider signing up for an online class. Check the Web site for your local college or university but consider other colleges and universities as well. Remember, it's an online class, so you aren't confined to a geographic area for studying.

DO LUNCH

As handy as electronic communication is, it's still no substitute for good old-fashioned human contact. And it's all too easy to fall into the habit of eating every meal in front of the computer screen. For this reason, home-based entrepreneurs need to make a point of scheduling people into their workweeks. Arrange to have lunch with a client, prospect, friend, or colleague on a regular basis. By scheduling time with people away from your house, you can break up your routine while giving yourself something to look forward to. If the person you meet is also home-based, you can take advantage of an extra benefit—you can go when the restaurant is less crowded.

JOIN ORGANIZATIONS

Organizations provide you with the opportunity to dramatically expand your business and social circles. There are dozens or even hundreds of different groups in your area. Each has its own purpose, rules, and benefits. For these reasons, you should belong to two or three different organizations. What organizations could you join?

- Your local Chamber of Commerce
- A local home-based business group
- A trade or professional organization
- A leads group
- A service club
- A special interest group

Let's take a look at each one's value to you as a business owner alone in your home office.

Chamber of Commerce

The mission of a Chamber of Commerce is to improve the economic climate in a particular geographic area. To this end, Chambers offer a wide range of activities and programs, including seminars, marketing opportunities, counseling, business discounts, and networking events. *Especially* networking events.

Chambers typically have anywhere from 5 to 20 networking events a month. These events can be anything from breakfasts to lunches to blenders after typical office hours. Therefore, you can choose events you want to attend, according to your schedule.

Chamber membership fees vary, based primarily on the size of the geographic location they serve and the activities they offer. Most set a fee scale based on number of employees in a business. Since you are the only person (at this point) involved in the business, you'll pay the lowest membership fee.

If the fee seems a little high for you at this point, ask if they accept payment over a period of time. You usually have the option of charging your membership fee. Chapter 5, "Piggy Banks and Megabanks," covered securing a business credit card. If you haven't applied for one yet, now would be the time to do so.

Interacting with others in the Chamber will help you build your confidence and bring you business, in addition to overcoming the isolation of a home-based business.

Home-Based Business Groups

Home-based business groups are not typical in every area as yet, but check with the Chamber of Commerce in your area to see if their home-based business members are meeting as a separate group. If not, ask how many home-based business owners they have as members. There may be some interest in starting a group, and your inquiry may provide the impetus to get it going. If you're already a member of that Chamber, talk with other home-based business members at some of the other networking events about interest in starting a group.

One of the greatest advantages to meeting with a home-based business group is knowing that these other business owners are sharing the same joys and concerns you have about living and working under the same roof. Talking with other home-based business owners about how they handle isolation, family situations, and the balance between work and personal life will energize you and help you overcome obstacles to your success.

If there is no group and you find enough interest from other home-based business owners to form one, there are some things you can do to get a group started.

If you're a member of the Chamber or other small business group, ask if there is a meeting room you can use. Advertise the meeting in the group newsletter. Put up flyers at your local bookstore, supermarket, and other community bulletin boards advertising an organizational meeting.

Get together with the other home-based business owners who showed initial interest and brainstorm what the group mission should be. Do you want a group that meets for a meal at a local restaurant as an informal networking group? Do you want to have informational meetings where you would invite someone to speak on business topics? Do you want a combination of these two or other ideas?

Bev helped start a home-based business group within her Chamber of Commerce. With the Chamber's support, notices were sent out to all members about the purpose of the group and a meeting time. Over a period of months, the group met to hear a speaker on subjects that would be of interest to any small business owner. After the speaker presented the topic, everyone had a chance to present a brief introduction of their business and pass out business cards. Drawings for door prizes donated by various members from business cards of those in attendance were an added benefit. The Chamber provided coffee and snacks during an informal networking time. As members began to know each other better, they referred business to one another and received referrals. For Bev, it became not only a way to get away from the home office for a few hours, but a sharing of ideas and business leads. (Chapters 10 and 14 go into more detail about the benefits of this type of networking.)

Trade and Professional Organizations

Another group you should belong to is the organization in your field. The *Gale's Directory of Associations* lists thousands of trade and professional organizations worldwide and can be found in the reference section of your local library. There is an organization for virtually any field you can think of. Some have chapters you can join. The benefit to joining the organization in your field, particularly one with a local chapter, is the opportunity to get away from the home office and meet with your peers to share and learn what's new in your field. Even if there is no local chapter, you may be able to find other members in your area through the national headquarters office.

Leads Groups

We discussed leads groups in Chapter 10. If you have the type of business that is easily referred (i.e., one that is not highly specialized and thus can be used by lots of different people) and if you can commit to the weekly or biweekly meetings, then a leads group can be a great way to get some regular social interaction while acquiring new prospects for your business. You can find leads groups through your local Chamber of Commerce, by talking with other business owners, or on the Web.

Service Clubs

The purpose of organizations such as Rotary, Lions, Kiwanis, Optimists, Jaycees, and Knights of Columbus is to provide some type of volunteer service to local communities. And great networking is a happy by-product of organized service. As a result, a service club is a terrific place to meet people and build friendships. While it can be a business opportunity, don't approach it that way. Join a club for the service and the fellowship. If your focus is in the right place—that is, the goals of the group—then people will naturally want to do business with you.

Wherever you live, odds are you have a multitude of service clubs in your area. Choose a group whose mission and values appeal to you. You can find clubs in your local yellow pages, through your Chamber of Commerce, or on the Web. Like lead-sharing groups, service clubs usually meet weekly or biweekly, although it may be for breakfast, lunch, or dinner. Also like lead-sharing groups, they often enforce attendance requirements, so understand the commitment involved.

Special Interest Groups

Finally, there are a host of other organizations whose purpose is not business-oriented, yet provide excellent opportunities to get out of your house and meet people. They include:

- Toastmasters International
- Alumni associations
- Sport and hobby clubs
- Book clubs
- Men's organizations
- Women's organizations
- Your child's PTA
- Your local homeowners association
- Your church, synagogue, or mosque

As with service clubs, focus on the business of the group rather than your business. Look at these groups primarily as opportunities for socializing. Any business you get from your relationships with other members is a bonus.

How to Make Your Membership Worthwhile

With any and all of these groups, several rules apply. Check them out before you join to make sure the group is a good fit for you. After you have written your membership check, attend meetings and events regularly. And to get the biggest return on your investment, raise your profile and credibility by volunteering for projects and committees.

Bev's first home-based business was a desktop publishing business. In order to get known, she joined her local Chamber of Commerce and a women's business owners group and then volunteered to work on the newsletters and other publications. She made announcements about items for the newsletters at meetings and wrote some of the articles as well.

Her name became associated with the newsletter, and other members got to know her through her volunteer work. An added benefit was that each month the members had a sample of her work in their mail. As a result, she began getting inquiries about her business.

Don is a member of three different Chambers of Commerce and since 1998 has been a member of the National Speakers Association. Over the years, he's been a member of Toastmasters, his college alumni association, and many other local groups. He has served on boards, committees, and task forces and is a frequent volunteer in his various organizations.

Our volunteer activities have helped us in three ways. First, they've improved our business skills by forcing us to get better at many of the items we listed in Chapter 8. Second, they've resulted in new clients for us as others have seen our work and gotten to know us. And third, they've given us a tremendous sense of accomplishment and satisfaction, separate from our businesses.

VOLUNTEER IN YOUR COMMUNITY

Another benefit to being a home-based business owner with control over your hours is your ability to volunteer in your community. In Chapter 1 we mentioned the ability to volunteer at your children's school or recreational program. There are many other organizations that also need volunteers, and you may now have the time and ability to schedule volunteer hours other than evenings and weekends. Some home-based business owners take a break in the middle of the day to deliver Meals-on-Wheels to the homebound. Others have volunteered to answer phones for small nonprofits for an hour or two a week. Your scheduling flexibility is a tremendous asset, enabling you to volunteer for a cause that's important to you while still taking care of your business.

BEWARE OF OVERCOMMITMENT

There is a dark side, however. One of the dangers of becoming involved in volunteer work, particularly in the early stages of your business, is overcommitment. Organizations generally have fewer volunteers than they would like to have. Once you volunteer for one thing, you may find yourself being asked to do more.

The volunteer work allows other business owners to get to know you, and will hopefully bring you new clients for your business. But you can easily find yourself overcommitted. You may find yourself balancing not only your personal life and your business, but your volunteer work as well. Suddenly dropping the volunteer work because you're too busy with clients can work against you with the organization. By not becoming overcommitted in the first place, you can probably find the right balance and become known as a reliable volunteer who keeps a commitment.

You may never completely replace the atmosphere and camaraderie fostered by your old water cooler. But incorporating some of these strategies into your day will stimulate you, challenge you, and perhaps increase business as well.

Chapter 12

MAKING IT
A FAMILY AFFAIR

How to Work with
and around Your Family

One of the most rewarding aspects to running a business from home is the opportunity to spend more time with your family. In this day and age when so many families complain about never being able to spend time together, a home-based business can be a major improvement in the entire family's lifestyle just by enabling you to spend more time at home with them. If other family members work in your business with you, that can be even better. After all, who better to partner with or hire than your own flesh-and-blood?

Unfortunately, family and business don't always mix easily. Layering a working relationship on top of a family relationship can be tricky. In this chapter we'll discuss some issues you need to be aware of in order to work with family members.

LAYING THE FOUNDATION

As with any issue involving relationships, the first step is communicating effectively. As we mentioned in Chapter 3, it's important to sit down with your entire family as you're devising your business plan. Because your business will share the same roof that they do, they'll have the capacity to affect your business whether they're working in it or not.

Your Spouse

What do you expect of your spouse or partner in relation to your business? What can your spouse expect from you? A business in the home can bring two people closer together or it can place a tremendous strain on a relationship.

Your spouse may not understand your desire to start your own business. He or she may fear the financial risk and the potential loss of income. Or your partner may fear that because running your own business can require more time than you used to work at your job, you'll be less accessible. Jealousy can be an issue if your spouse perceives that your business is more important to you than he or she is. Alternatively, your spouse may feel that since you're going to be home all the time now, you can take care of much of the housework and family chores.

On the other hand, your spouse may be excited at the prospect of you being home more, and may even want to be involved in the business with you. Either way, talking about each other's hopes, fears, and expectations will result in your getting better support from your partner than you would otherwise.

Your Children

Depending on their age, attitudes, and aptitudes, your children can be great for your business, and vice versa. Working with you, your kids can learn important lessons about responsibility and the value of a good work ethic. Even if they're not directly involved in your business, seeing you and talking with you can give them an early understanding of business, time management, economics, negotiating, and more.

On the other hand, your home-based business can potentially create the same kinds of friction with your kids that it can with your spouse. Your children may not take your business seriously. They may become jealous and frustrated because of the hours you put in. Children—younger children especially—often can't understand that although you're home, you can't devote time to them.

Involving them in your business planning as well, even if they will not be working in the business, can help allay their fears and give them an understanding of how your business fits in the household.

When Bev became home-based in 1987, her teenage son resented that she was now there when he came home from school. He was used to having the house to himself for several hours. When he became interested in developing his own motorcycle helmet painting business, however, having Mom at home to help him became an advantage.

Not too many years later, Bev's husband was forced into early retirement and decided to open his own handyman business from the house. Bev's experience and knowledge of home-based business helped him, and there were now three businesses being run from the house. Each different, each in a different part of the house, but all compatible; what Bev started grew into a family affair.

Although Bev didn't hire her family to work for her, numerous family members have helped in her business and with household duties when she was on deadline. After her father passed away and her mother came to live with them, Bev's mother helped by doing mailings as well as taking over some of the cooking and cleaning. And remember her mother-in-law, who was dying but managed to give Bev tremendous help in her business. None of them had a full understanding of her business efforts prior to their involvement.

WORKING WITH YOUR FAMILY

Employing family members can be both beneficial and risky. On the positive side, you get an employee whom you've known for a long time (possibly since birth!). You know their strengths and weaknesses, their work habits and their trustworthiness. On the negative side, managing a family member can be difficult. We tolerate actions we wouldn't stand for from an ordinary employee. If the family member is being paid a below-market wage—or none at all—it's extremely hard to enforce instructions. And nobody wants to have to fire his or her spouse or child. So let's look at how to avoid that situation and work effectively with different types of family members.

Your Spouse

A business relationship is different than a marital relationship, and in order for you and your spouse to work together without killing each other, it's important to define both relationships, so that each partner knows what to expect from the other. Will you two be business partners or will your spouse merely be your employee? What kinds of responsibilities will you each have? And how will you resolve business disputes and prevent them from affecting your personal relationship?

One approach that can help is to review the section on partnerships in Chapter 3. Since your marriage is a partnership, whether or not your business is, it can be beneficial to draw up a partnership agreement with your spouse in order to work through the relevant issues ahead of time.

Your Children

Your kids can potentially be a source of flexible and trustworthy (and cheap!) labor, enabling you to leverage your time without breaking the bank.

In return, working in your company—even occasional part-time work—can provide them with skills and experiences that will give them an advantage in whatever direction they pursue. But there are a couple of keys to making sure your kids and your company get along.

First, never force your children to be involved with your business, especially at younger ages. Kids need time to be kids. And anything they're pushed into will likely be a focus for resentment. There's no point having an employee slouching sullenly around your office wishing they were anywhere but there.

The second key is to match tasks and pay to their age and abilities. Young children may not be able to go out and make sales calls, but they can have fun attaching stamps and labels to envelopes. And they'll happily do it for nothing or perhaps a token gift. As your kids get older, give them opportunities to expand their skills without overwhelming them, and pay them accordingly.

Your Parents

Hiring parents or older relatives who live with you or near you can be a huge boon for you, especially if they have previous business experience. You get the benefit of their knowledge, skills, and hard-earned lessons. At the same time, they can stay productive and useful, contributing to their sense of well-being and giving them a purpose. And a flexible schedule means they don't have to push themselves too hard.

The pitfall you have to watch out for is the "I'm in charge" syndrome. Parents can sometimes have difficulty taking direction from their children, no matter how much you've grown. So initially—at the time of hiring—you need to be specific about precisely what their responsibility and authority will be.

A LITTLE RESPECT

With all three types of family members, it's important that everyone agree to respect the business, each other, and the needs of customers. Just as most families have "house rules" that govern behavior in the home, so your business needs "business rules" that govern behavior in the home business. Get everyone's input into what the rules should be and then hold everyone accountable for following them. You want your home-business environment to be relaxed, enjoyable, and flexible, and at the same time, you need the atmosphere to be conducive to work, so that it will get done.

Above all, keep the lines of communication open. Provide positive and constructive feedback on a regular basis. And do your best to treat everyone as fairly as possible. Follow the above guidelines and you and your family can live—and work—happily ever after.

Chapter 13
WHERE DO I GO FROM HERE?
Planning for Growth

If you've ever had a job interview, you've probably heard the question, "Where do you want to be in five years?" Now that you're starting your own home-based business, you need to ask that question of yourself. Because once you've passed the survival stage and made your business profitable, you're going to have some choices to make. And the earlier you start thinking about those choices, the easier they'll be to make.

In this chapter, we'll explore some of the issues related to growth. Our goal is primarily to get you thinking about your possibilities, pitfalls, and priorities.

YOUR TWO MAJOR RISKS

There are two major risks in running your home-based business. One is that you won't have enough customers to survive. The other is that you'll end up with too many customers to serve properly.

The first risk seems obvious and straightforward: not enough customers, not enough money to pay the bills, so the business has to shut down. This is the challenge that occupies your complete attention in the start-up phase, and usually the first few years, of your business.

The second risk can be harder to grasp, but is equally dangerous. If you can't give your customers the quality, service, and results you promised them, they'll find somebody else. And a dissatisfied customer who switches can be nearly impossible to win back. You almost certainly have a personal list of businesses that you will *never* buy from again because of bad experiences. And there's probably nothing they can do to change your mind.

The second risk poses another potential problem as well. One of the reasons you wanted to start your own business was that you didn't want to work insanely long hours under highly stressful conditions. When you have more business than you can handle, that's precisely the position you're left in.

In order to maintain the lifestyle that's important to you, you have to plan for what to do if and when your business generates more business than you can currently deal with. And that gets back to your long-term business and lifestyle goals.

YOUR GOALS

So what would you like your business to look like five years from now? Ten years? Twenty?

Do you still want to be working at home? And if so, do you want your home office to look basically the way it does now or completely different?

Do you want to continue to work by yourself or would you rather spend more time in the manager and leader roles we described in Chapter 8? How big a workforce do you want to manage?

Will your kids be involved in the business? Will they have moved out of the house? Will your parents move in?

Do you want to keep your business small and easily manageable or would you prefer to build it into a big company? Are you committed to your business for life or will you want to sell it at some point?

Because some of the options available to you require major decisions, it's best to think about these questions in advance. That way you can prepare strategies that will make it easier to manage your growth. Since growth is so often erratic and unpredictable, managing it is the key to keeping your business healthy and yourself sane.

MANAGING GROWTH

What do we mean by *growth*? An increase in demand for your products and services. Growth is a healthy thing for your business so long as you can effectively service your customers.

When your demand increases beyond your ability to handle it, you have four basic choices:

1. You can raise your prices.
2. You can turn away new customers.

3. You can refer the extra business to other companies.
4. You can increase your capacity to handle the additional work.

Raising Your Prices

Because running a business from home requires less overhead, many home-based entrepreneurs pass the cost savings directly to customers. When the business delivers quality work at below-market prices, demand can jump. In such an instance, one of the best, fastest, and most flexible courses of action is raising your prices. Increasing prices to meet or exceed the average price of the market typically does two things simultaneously: It slows your demand and increases your profit on every transaction.

Depending on your business, you can raise your fees temporarily to account for seasonal demand, raise your prices on only certain products or services, or raise your rates for new customers while keeping existing customers at their previous rates.

However, raising your prices can have an unintended—and ironic—side effect: It can increase the perceived value of your goods and services in the eyes of your customers and prospects, thus *increasing* demand. So if you keep raising your rates and the new customers just keep coming (which is not a bad problem to have), you'll need to employ another tactic as well, which is next on our list.

Turning Away New Customers

Nobody likes to refuse business from a new customer, but sometimes you have to. If a business makes promises to a customer and doesn't deliver, it has likely lost that customer forever. And the average upset customer tells nine people about their negative experience.

If instead you're honest with your prospect about your inability to serve them properly (even though you'd *love* to have them as a customer), you'll earn their respect. That in turn can buy you a second chance later on.

Referring Your Competitors

If you have to turn potential customers away, there is an additional action you can take to ensure a more favorable outcome for both you and your prospect: Refer them to one of your competitors. Lest you think we're out of our minds, let us explain.

If you "just say no" to your potential customer, they will of course take their business to another company, where they may have a good or a bad experience. But if you refer them to one of your competitors, who you know does great work, they will almost certainly have a positive experience. As a result, they'll be grateful to you for steering them in the right direction. At the same time, your competitor will be grateful to you for the referral. So while you may not have a sale, you do have two advocates.

Increasing Your Capacity

Your fourth option, increasing your capacity to handle more business, is the one that requires the most planning and effort. It's a long-term solution that has a significant impact on you, your home, and your family. So you and your family need to discuss the possibilities and agree on courses of action before the time comes to actually start making changes.

Increasing your capacity can mean any or all of the following:

- Freeing up additional office and work space
- Increasing storage space
- Improving shipping capacity
- Installing additional phone lines
- Increasing the number of distribution channels
- Acquiring lines of credit
- Finding additional help
- Moving the business out of the home

If you need more space in your home, you can build an addition onto your house or you may even consider moving to a larger home. With home-based businesses becoming more popular, builders have been designing homes with office space from the ground up, and prewiring new homes for extra phone and computer lines.

The Greek philosopher Heraclitus once asserted, "There is nothing permanent except change." Your company, your family, and your priorities will all undergo dramatic change as your business grows. Fortunately, by planning ahead, you can direct the change, rather than having it direct you.

Chapter 14

EMPLOYEES OR INDEPENDENT CONTRACTORS?

How to Determine Which Is Right for Your Business

Some home-based business owners make a decision early on to not have employees. They will only take on as much business as they can handle by themselves. Other home-based entrepreneurs either know from the beginning that they'll want and need employees, or they find themselves with so much business that they decide they need to hire some.

Regardless of your current thinking about having employees in your home-based business, there may come a time when you decide you need help. Here are some of the most common reasons:

- Your business has increased beyond a one-person operation.
- You want to bid on a larger project than you can handle by yourself.
- You hate doing _____ (fill in the blank).
- You feel isolated and want the presence of another person in your office.
- You feel one or more additional people will make you look bigger, thus increasing the perceived value of your business.
- You need expertise in an area you don't personally possess.
- You need to relieve yourself of menial tasks to free up time to do more of what you do best.

Help can come in different forms. You can hire employees, either to work full- or part-time, in your office or from their own home. You can hire other businesses. Or you can subcontract work to other home-based or small businesses, or team up with another business. Given the choice you make, you might have to know the difference between an independent subcontractor and an employee. The answer's important, since it has tax implications.

Let's look at some of these possibilities and distinctions.

HIRING EMPLOYEES

Let's start with hiring employees. Previously in this book, we talked about zoning. This is the first consideration before hiring an employee for your home-based business, because some localities prohibit people working in other people's homes unless they are related to the homeowner. Other localities restrict the number of on-site employees a home-based business may have. And still other localities have no restrictions at all.

Let's assume your local zoning ordinance allows you to have one or more employees in your home. Now the decision is whether you have room for an employee, and if you want him or her to work in your home office. Ask yourself these questions:

- Is there space for another desk?
- Is there enough room for two (or more) people to work and move around comfortably?
- Will you need another telephone or computer?
- What if you want to meet with a client in your office? Is there a place for the employee to go while you meet with the client?
- How comfortable are you with someone else being in your house while you're away from the office?
- How comfortable are you with someone else being alone with your kids while you're away from the office?
- Can you secure your personal space from your office space?
- Is there a bathroom close by the office space or would your employee have to use a bathroom normally used by household members?
- Do you prefer quiet when you work?
- Do you keep irregular business hours?
- How do you dress while you're in your home office?
- How do you expect an employee to dress in your home office?
- Will you give the employee a key to your house?
- Is there parking space for another car?

As you can see, there are a lot of issues to consider. Bringing an outsider into your home changes everything, assuming it's even practical. Many home-based business owners either aren't comfortable having an employee working in their home office or don't have sufficient space.

If you *are* comfortable, however, and you have the space, you then have a whole new set of questions to consider as you determine how best to fill the need you have. Ask yourself:

- Do I need full-time help or just part-time?
- Do I need someone every day or just a few days a week?
- What exactly needs to be done?
- Will this need be temporary or permanent?
- Does this position require skilled or unskilled labor?
- If skilled, how skilled and in what areas?
- How much can I afford to pay someone?
- How much will an employee save me or earn me?

As you determine the answers to these questions, write a detailed job description. Include the responsibilities of the position and the skills necessary to achieve them. Be clear about the level of authority the person filling the position will have. You can adjust the job description as your business and the number of employees grow, as long as the adjustments are mutually agreed to.

One pitfall to be wary of is mixing in personal tasks with business tasks. Unless you're specifically hiring a personal assistant to take care of your personal needs, steer clear of having your employees take on household duties. Remember, your employee works for the *company,* not you personally.

Once you've developed the job description, the next step is to create a written employment agreement. Preparing one before you start interviewing candidates will give you time to do it right. Be sure to include such elements as:

- Job title and responsibilities
- Types of duties to be performed
- Hours and days to be worked
- Location where work will be performed
- Compensation and how often it will be paid
- Benefits, if any
- Vacation policies
- Policies regarding sick days and personal days (yours and theirs)

- Holidays and whether they are paid
- Expense reimbursement policies
- Performance review procedures
- Disciplinary procedures
- Termination and resignation guidelines
- Disability contingencies
- Dispute-resolution procedures
- Confidentiality agreement
- Noncompete agreement

With regard to sick days and personal days, you will need to develop a policy regarding your own time off. Will you require your employee to take time off at the same time you do? If you are ill, do you want your employee coming to the home office or will he or she not work that day? A whole new set of issues arises when you are working from a home office with employees.

Where to Find Good Employees

Now that you know exactly what you're looking for, the next question becomes who to hire. This is a critically important issue, because hiring a great employee can be the best thing that ever happens to your business, while hiring a poor employee can be disastrous. Don once hired somebody for his courier business despite having some reservations about the applicant he couldn't quite put his finger on. In the short space of time the employee was with the company, he did damage that took almost a year to correct. So hiring the right person is paramount.

Perhaps you already have someone in mind. It might be a neighbor, a friend, or a family member. Somebody you already know, like, and trust is certainly preferable. After all, this employee will have access to your business information and will also be aware of your household activities. So if you have someone in mind, definitely ask whether he or she would be interested.

However, you should never pressure someone or make them feel obligated to accept your offer. A friend or relative can be hesitant to turn you down for fear of damaging the relationship. So make it clear that you won't take a rejection personally. Also be clear about the effect a business relationship may have on your personal relationship with a friend or family member. As an employee, he or she will need to take direction from you as well as accept your final say in how things are done. And there is always the possibility that at some point you'll have to let an employee go.

If you're going to hire a stranger instead, you have two challenges: First, finding good candidates, and second, screening them to select the best one for your business. The first task is fairly straightforward. There are lots of options for finding potential employees, including:

- Classified ads
- Online job sites
- High schools
- Colleges
- Retirement centers
- Employment agencies
- Temporary agencies
- Friends and colleagues

As you find candidates, have them provide you with their résumés and then call the applicants who most interest you. Conduct a thorough phone interview first. Make it clear that your business is home-based and determine how comfortable the applicant is with the idea of working in your home. This may not be the work situation your job seeker had in mind, so he or she may need to think long and hard about it. Discuss both the benefits and challenges of working in a home-based business so he or she fully understands both and can make a good decision. You don't want a person you've just hired to decide after two weeks that this is not the right environment.

If, after the phone interview, you and the applicant both decide you'd like to move forward, invite the candidate to your home for a second interview. This will enable both of you to get a better feel for each other and make a better determination of whether this is the right fit. If you're not completely comfortable with someone, for any reason, don't hire the person. Listen to both your brain and your gut.

One of the keys to effective interviewing is asking the right questions. For ideas, check out the book *The Manager's Book of Questions: 751 Great Interview Questions for Hiring the Best Person* by John Kador. Create a list of the questions that are most appropriate for your situation and ask those questions consistently of every candidate.

Before you extend a job offer to someone—whether you're hiring a part-time or full-time employee—check out references and former employers. It's especially important to do your due diligence when hiring for a home-based business. Doing a criminal background check is worthwhile, particularly if you don't know this person at all. There are many services online that can help you do a background check on a potential employee for a reasonable cost. It's definitely money well spent, because hiring mistakes are among the most costly errors that business owners make.

Temporary Help

If you're considering hiring a temp through an agency, you may find that temp agencies are reluctant to send workers to a home-based office. Those agencies that do will usually require a separate entrance to the office, at a minimum.

Also keep in mind that temporary workers are extremely expensive because you're paying not just their wage, but also the temp agency's fees. On the other hand, using temps gives you the chance to "try out" people to find one who is a good fit for you and your business. When you find someone you really like, you can offer him or her a permanent position with your company. Another benefit of using temp workers is that they are typically prescreened by the temp agency, although you should always double-check.

Help from Outside the Office

Perhaps you decide that you don't have room for an employee in your home office, or that you don't want someone else coming into your home. There are other options, depending on your business and your needs.

Because so many people want to work from home, you may be able to find someone who is willing to work from his own home as your employee. If your need is for a typist, a bookkeeper, or a researcher, this work might not have to be done from your office. Your employee wouldn't even have to come to you if you didn't want him to—you could deliver the work to him at his office. This employee could be your teleworker. As in any teleworking situation, you need to have a level of trust with your employee, a time frame for accomplishing the work, and knowledge of his skills and ability to complete the work.

Don't forget: Now that you're an employer, you also have to do additional paperwork. You will be responsible for employment taxes and additional insurance. Speak with an accountant about your responsibilities as an employer. It may not be worth what it costs in time and money to hire an employee.

HIRING OTHER BUSINESSES

Another way to get the work done is to hire another business owner to do it for you. This is where your networking will come in handy. As you get to know other business owners, you'll familiarize yourself with their skills as well as what they charge. You will come to know the ones that others use for their businesses, which will serve as a reference.

Perhaps your business is doing well but you don't have time to do the bookkeeping, billing, or designing of your marketing materials. Hiring another business to do these tasks will free up more hours for you to devote to your expertise, and it will be more cost effective as well. For instance, if you're a consultant who charges $150 an hour and you spend two to three hours a week doing bookkeeping and billing, that's $300 to $450 you might have been earning as a consultant. A bookkeeper/billing clerk might charge you $35 to $50 an hour and be able to accomplish the tasks much quicker. Do the math. We think you'll agree this makes good business sense.

INDEPENDENT CONTRACTOR VERSUS EMPLOYEE

Perhaps you need help so you can take on larger projects. In this case, your need might not be for an employee but for subcontractors. Bev had a situation like this several years ago. A nonprofit group that produced a bimonthly newsletter of school events for teachers in the local school system contacted her. They wanted someone to coordinate the whole project, which included attending the event and writing a story about it, taking pictures, and laying out a newsletter with the stories, pictures, and other graphics.

Through contacts in the business groups Bev belonged to, she found a writer and a photographer to whom she could subcontract those pieces of the project. She received the bid and produced the newsletter for two years with the help of her two independent contractors. Bev would not have received the contract without this help.

In the courier business that Don and his father ran, all the delivery drivers were independent contractors, which is the norm in the industry. They advertised the positions in the Help Wanted section of the classifieds and explained to each applicant what was involved in being a contractor and how that differed from being an employee.

Here's where the tax implications can come into it: The Internal Revenue Service prefers that your help be classified as employees. You and perhaps your help probably prefer to have them classified as independent contractors. Make sure you know the difference, because the penalties for the wrong classification can be devastating for your business finances. Here are some guidelines to help you.

Independent Contractor

If your worker earns more than $600 and qualifies as a genuine independent contractor, you prepare a tax form at the end of the year called the IRS Form 1099 Misc., stating the amount you paid the worker. Preparing and sending that form is essentially all that's necessary.

Employee

If your worker is really an employee, you have to deduct and withhold federal income taxes, pay social security taxes, unemployment taxes, and perhaps fringe benefits. The administrative and tax burden tempts many small business owners to call a worker an independent contractor, whether the worker qualifies as one or not.

The IRS strongly disfavors independent contractors. It claims that more than $20 billion in uncollected taxes is lost to it each year. It has therefore imposed strict regulations that can cost the employer stiff penalties, fines, back taxes, and interest charges.

Determining Which Is Which

How do you determine whether a person can be classified as an independent contractor? There are no specific rules, but rather, a set of factors that the IRS uses to determine the worker's classification. No one factor determines the relationship; the relationship is looked at as a whole.

Control

One of the main factors is that of control; that is, how much control you have over your worker. The general rule is that if you control or have the right to control only the *results* of the work and not the means or methods of accomplishing the work, then the worker might be considered an independent contractor. You can set the standards, but you may not control *how* the work is done as well.

If you require the worker to work on your premises, set a work schedule, have the worker use your tools, and you have the right to fire him or her, these are all indications of an employer-employee relationship. On the other hand, if a worker comes to you, picks up a project, goes off, completes the project without your oversight, and returns it to you, they will probably be considered an independent contractor.

Permanency of Relationship

Another of the main factors in determining what working category a person falls into is the permanency of the relationship. The worker who is hired for an indefinite period of time might more likely be considered an employee. If the worker is engaged for a specific project with a distinct beginning and end, there is more indication that he or she is an independent contractor, especially if the worker hires him- or herself out to others for similar services and has different clients. This was the case for Bev's independent contractors.

Role of Services Rendered

Yet another factor is the extent to which the services rendered are integral to your business. In other words, if the worker is hired to support or do similar work to what you do, it is an indication of employment. If the person comes to set up your office or rewire your house, he or she would be considered an independent contractor, especially if the services are offered to the general public.

Opportunity for Loss

And the final significant factor is the opportunity for loss. If the worker bears the risk of using his own initiative, judgment, and foresight, and has expenses that are reimbursable only by special arrangement, it is an indication of the independent contractor designation. If the worker has no chance to lose money, then there's every chance that he or she may be deemed an employee.

In Bev's case, if the independent contractors didn't perform their work, they didn't get paid. There was also no provision in their agreement to reimburse them for expenses incurred. The photographer paid for his own film, camera, and development. If the camera broke, the photographer was responsible for having it repaired at his own expense. Neither independent contractor was specifically reimbursed for travel expenses.

Consider now the 20 common law factors used by the IRS to determine a worker's classification.

20 Common Law Factors Used by the IRS to Determine a Worker's Classification

Workers are generally considered employees if they:

1. Must comply with employers' instructions about their work
2. Receive training from or at the direction of the employer
3. Provide services that are integrated into the business
4. Provide services that must be rendered personally

5. Hire, supervise, and pay assistants for the employee
6. Have an ongoing working relationship with the employer
7. Must follow set hours of work
8. Work full-time for an employer
9. Do their work on the employers' premises
10. Must do their work in a sequence set by the employer
11. Must submit regular reports to the employer
12. Receive payments of regular amounts at set intervals
13. Receive payments for business and/or travel expenses
14. Rely on the employer to furnish tools and materials
15. Lack a major investment in facilities used to perform the service
16. Cannot make a profit or suffer a loss from their services
17. Work for one employer at a time
18. Do not offer their services to the general public
19. Can be fired by the employer
20. May quit work at any time without incurring liability

Written Agreement or Just a Handshake?

The IRS looks closely at independent contractor situations and has the power to reclassify subcontractors to employee status *retroactively*. Criminal charges can also be brought against you, the business owner. Employee taxes, penalties, and fines can break your business. It is essential that you have a written agreement clearly showing the contractor as independent of you and your business.

A lawyer specializing in small businesses can help you draw up an independent contractor agreement that covers you and your contractor. In addition, it may also be necessary to have a written agreement with the client that clearly states a teaming arrangement on the project. (See Chapter 1 for information on finding a lawyer.)

FINDING HELP

In Chapter 12 we discussed making your business a family affair. If you skipped that chapter or don't remember what you read, this might be a good time to go back and read it. There are a lot of advantages to having your family work with you in the business. There are also some disadvantages. But the disadvantages might be outweighed by the disadvantages of having an employee.

If you've decided not to hire someone outside your family to work in the business, but you see subcontracting or teaming up as a means to your end, your networking skills will come in handy in finding this help.

As you network at business meetings, social events, and so on, you want to get to know other business owners as people you can call on for subcontracting or teaming up. Your gut instinct about a person you've just met is generally a good guide to follow, but ask questions as well about the person's work, clients, and future plans for their business (see discussion on networking in Chapter 10).

A wonderful resource for learning more about teaming up with other business owners to expand your business is the book *Teaming Up* by Paul and Sarah Edwards and Rick Benzel. In addition to details about different teaming arrangements, the book includes templates for writing your own agreements.

BUT WAIT, THERE'S MORE!

Additional Home-Based Business Resources You Should Know About

BOOKS
Getting Started

Brabec, Barbara. *Creative Cash: How to Profit From Your Special Artistry, Creativity, Hand Skills, and Related Know-How*. Prima Lifestyles, 1998.

———. *Handmade for Profit! Hundreds of Secrets to Success in Selling Arts and Crafts*. M. Evans & Co, 2002.

———. *Homemade Money: Starting Smart! How to Turn Your Talents, Experience, and Know-How into a Profitable Home-Based Business That's Perfect for You!* M. Evans & Co, 2003.

Edwards, Paul, and Sarah Edwards. *The Best Home Businesses for the 21st Century*. J.P. Tarcher, 1999.

———. *Making Money with Your Computer at Home*. Putnam, 1997.

Edwards, Paul, Sarah Edwards, and Walter Zooi. *Home Businesses You Can Buy*. J.P. Tarcher, 1997.

Huff, Pricilla. *101 Best Home-Based Businesses for Women*. Prima Lifestyles, 1998.

Lonier, Terri. *Working Solo*. John Wiley & Sons, 1998.

McQuown, Judith H. *Inc. Yourself: How to Profit by Setting Up Your Own Corporation*. Career Press, 2004.

Nathan, Karen B., and Alice Magos. *Incorporate! An Easy Step-by-Step Plan for Entrepreneurs*. McGraw-Hill, 2003.

Weltman, Barbara. *The Complete Idiot's Guide to Starting a Home-Based Business*. Alpha Books, 2000.

Hiring

Kador, John. *The Manager's Book of Questions: 751 Great Interview Questions for Hiring the Best Person.* McGraw-Hill, 1997.

Yate, Martin. *Hiring the Best: A Manager's Guide to Effective Interviewing.* Adams Media, 1997.

Home Office Organization

Kanarek, Lisa. *101 Home Office Success Secrets.* Career Press, 2000.

———. *Home Office Life: Making a Space to Work at Home.* Rockport Publishers, 2001.

———. *Home Office Solutions.* Rockport Publishers, 2004.

———. *Organizing Your Home Business.* Made EZ Products, 2002.

Inspiration and Insights

Blasingame, Jim. *Small Business Is Like a Bunch of Bananas.* Greenleaf Book Group, 2001.

Hill, Napoleon. *Think & Grow Rich.* Ballantine Books, 1987.

Kennedy, Dan. *No Rules: 21 Giant Lies about Success and How to Make It Happen Now.* Plume, 1998.

Pink, Daniel H. *Free Agent Nation: The Future of Working for Yourself.* Warner Books, 2002.

Marketing

Allen, Debbie. *Confessions of Shameless Self Promoters.* Success Showcase Publishing, 2002.

Brabec, Barbara. *Homemade Money: Bringing in the Bucks! A Business Management and Marketing Bible for Home-Business Owners, Self-Employed Individuals and Web Entrepreneurs Working from Home Base.* M. Evans & Co, 2003.

Cialdini, Robert. *Influence: The Psychology of Persuasion.* Quill, 1998.

Crandall, Rick. *1001 Ways to Market Your Services: Even If You Hate to Sell.* McGraw-Hill, 1998.

Davidson, Jeffrey. *Marketing for the Home-Based Business.* Adams Media Corp., 1999.

Edwards, Paul, and Sarah Edwards. *Getting Business to Come to You.* J.P. Tarcher, 1998.

Fletcher, Tana, and Julia Rockler. *Getting Publicity.* Self Counsel Press, 2000.

Godin, Seth. *Permission Marketing.* Simon & Schuster, 1999.

Kennedy, Dan. *The Ultimate Marketing Plan: Find Your Most Promotable Competitive Edge, Turn It into a Powerful Marketing Message, and Deliver It to the Right Prospects.* Adams Media, 2000.

Levinson, Jay Conrad. *Guerrilla Marketing.* Houghton Mifflin, 1998.

Levinson, Jay Conrad, Rick Frishman, and Jill Lublin. *Guerrilla Publicity.* Adams Media, 2002.

Levinson, Jay Conrad, and Seth Godin. *Guerrilla Marketing for the Home-Based Business.* Houghton Mifflin, 1995.

Levinson, Jay Conrad, Mark S. A. Smith, and Orvel Ray Wilson. *Guerrilla Trade Show Selling.* John Wiley & Sons, 1997.

McMurtry, Jeanette Maw. *Big Business Marketing for Small Business Budgets.* McGraw-Hill, 2003.

Money Issues

Carter, Gary. *J.K. Lasser's Taxes Made Easy for Your Home-Based Business.* John Wiley & Sons, 2002.

Kelly, Kate. *How to Set Your Fees and Get Them.* Visibility Enterprises, 1994.

Networking and Partnering

Burg, Bob. *Endless Referrals: Network Your Everyday Contacts into Sales.* McGraw Hill, 1998.

Cates, Bill. *Unlimited Referrals: Secrets That Turn Business Relationships into Gold.* Referral Coach International, 1996.

Edwards, Paul, Sarah Edwards, and Rick Benzel. *Teaming Up.* J.P. Tarcher, 1997.

RoAne, Susan. *How to Work a Room: The Ultimate Guide to Savvy Socializing in Person and Online.* Quill, 2000.

Parenting

Colby, Patricia, and Ellen Parlapiano. *Mompreneurs.* Perigree, 2002.

Edwards, Paul, Sarah Edwards, and Lisa M. Roberts. *The Entrepreneurial Parent: How to Earn Your Living and Still Enjoy Your Family, Your Work, and Your Life.* J.P. Tarcher, 2002.

Roberts, Lisa M. *How to Raise a Family and a Career under the Same Roof.* Bookhaven Press, 1997.

Sales

Gitomer, Jeffrey. *The Sales Bible.* John Wiley & Sons, 2003.

Heiman, Stephen E., and Diane Sanchez. *The New Strategic Selling.* Warner Books, 1998.

Kennedy, Dan S. *The Ultimate Sales Letter: Boost Your Sales with Powerful Sales Letters, Based on Madison Avenue Techniques.* Adams Media, 2000.

LeBoeuf, Michael. *How to Win Customers and Keep Them for Life.* Penguin Putnam, 2000.

Levinson, Jay Conrad, Mark S. A. Smith, and Orvel Ray Wilson. *Guerrilla TeleSelling: New Unconventional Weapons and Tactics to Get the Business When You Can't Be There in Person.* John Wiley & Sons, 1998.

Mandino, Og. *The Greatest Salesman in the World.* Bantam, 1983.

Penoyer, Flyn. *Teleselling Techniques That Close the Sale.* AMACOM, 1997.

Time Management

Allen, David. *Getting Things Done: The Art of Stress-Free Productivity.* Penguin, 2003.

Covey, Stephen R. *The Seven Habits of Highly Effective People.* Simon & Schuster, 1990.

Covey, Stephen R., A. Roger Merrill, and Rebecca R. Merrill. *First Things First.* Free Press, 1996.

WEB RESOURCES

Authors' Web Sites

Beverley Williams — www.BeverleyWilliams.com

Don Cooper — www.DonCooper.com

The 30-Second Commute — www.ThirtySecondCommute.com

Business Information and Ideas

Dun & Bradstreet	www.dnb.com
The Small Business Advocate	www.smallbusiness advocate.com

Government Agencies

Federal Trade Commission	www.ftc.gov
Internal Revenue Service	www.irs.gov
Small Business Administration (SBA)	www.sba.gov
SBA Office of Advocacy	www.sba.gov/advocacy
Small Business Development Centers (SBDCs)	www.sba.org/sbdc
U.S. Postal Service	www.usps.gov

Home Business Insurance

Cigna Property & Casualty	www.cigna.com
Fireman's Fund	www.the-fund.com
The Hartford	www.thehartford.com
Insurance Information Institute	www.iii.org
Travelers Property Casualty	www.travelers.com
Zurich Small Business	www.zurichsmall business.com

Magazines

Business 2.0	www.business20.com
Entrepreneur	www.entrepreneur mag.com
Fast Company	www.fastcompany.com
Home Business	www.homebusiness mag.com
Inc. Magazine	www.inc.com

Office Space

Executive Office Club	www.houroffice.com
Office Suites Plus	www.officesuitesplus.com

Office Supplies and Furnishings

Office Depot	www.officedepot.com
Office Max	www.officemax.com
Reliable Home Office	www.reliablehome office.com
Staples	www.staples.com

Organizations

American Association of Franchisees and Dealers	www.aafd.org
American Association of Home-Based Businesses	www.aahbb.org
At-Home Dad	www.athomedad.net
Direct Selling Association	www.dsa.org
Home-Based Working Moms	www.hbwm.com
International Franchise Organization	www.franchise.org
Mother's Home Business Network	www.homeworking mom.com
National Association for the Self-Employed	www.nase.org
National Association of Women Business Owners	www.nawbo.org
National Black Chamber of Commerce	www.nationalbcc.org
National Federation of Independent Businesses	www.nfib.com
National Small Business Council	www.nsbc.org
Service Corps of Retired Executives (SCORE)	www.score.org
U.S. Chamber of Commerce	www.uschamber.com
U.S. Hispanic Chamber of Commerce	www.ushcc.com
U.S. Pan Asian American Chamber of Commerce	www.uspaacc.com

Index

ABOUT THE AUTHORS

Beverley Williams is an internationally renowned author and speaker, and she is the founder of the American Association of Home-Based Businesses.

Don Cooper is an internationally acclaimed sales and marketing expert who has worked full-time from his home for more than a decade. He is the former home-based business columnist for *Small Business News Washington*.